RAND | NATIONAL DEFENSE RESEARCH INSTITUTE

T0308583

Achieving Peace in Northern Mali

Past Agreements, Local Conflicts, and the Prospects for a Durable Settlement

Stephanie Pezard, Michael Shurkin

Prepared for the Office of the Secretary of Defense, Office of African Affairs

For more information on this publication, visit www.rand.org/t/rr892

Library of Congress Cataloging-in-Publication Data

Pezard, Stephanie.
Achieving peace in northern Mali : past agreements, local conflicts, and the prospects for a
durable settlement / Stephanie Pezard, Michael Shurkin
    pages cm
Includes bibliographical references.
    ISBN 978-0-8330-8823-9 (pbk. : alk. paper)
1. Mali—History—Tuareg Rebellion, 2012- 2. Mal—History—Coup d'etat, 2012. 3.
Mali—Politics and government—1991- I. Shurkin, Michael Robert. II. Rand Corporation.
III. Title.
DT551.84.P49 2015
303.6'9096623—dc23   2015012292

Published by the RAND Corporation, Santa Monica, Calif.

© Copyright 2015 RAND Corporation

RAND® is a registered trademark

Cover image courtesy of Rebecca Zimmerman; used with permission.

Limited Print and Electronic Distribution Rights

The RAND Corporation is a research organization that develops solutions to public
policy challenges to help make communities throughout the world safer and more secure,
healthier and more prosperous. RAND is nonprofit, nonpartisan, and committed to the
public interest.

RAND's publications do not necessarily reflect the opinions of its research clients and sponsors.

Support RAND
Make a tax-deductible charitable contribution at
www.rand.org/giving/contribute

www.rand.org

Preface

This report examines the prospects for stabilization in Mali following the political and military crisis that began in 2012. In that perspective, it examines why past peace accords failed and the extent to which those failures can be attributed to poor implementation and lack of good will from Bamako (the most commonly heard explanation) or to the presence of "spoilers" among northern communities whose political interests clashed with those of other factions. The report highlights the key grievances that have yet to be effectively addressed and suggests ways to include them in future peace and security agreements. Finally, to identify lessons that might be applied to Mali, the report examines the factors behind the relative stability of Mali's neighbor Niger, which faces nearly all the same drivers of instability that Mali does.

This research was sponsored by the Office of African Affairs in the Office of the Secretary of Defense and conducted within the International Security and Defense Policy Center of the RAND National Defense Research Institute, a federally funded research and development center sponsored by the Office of the Secretary of Defense, the Joint Staff, the Unified Combatant Commands, the Navy, the Marine Corps, the defense agencies, and the defense Intelligence Community.

For more information on the International Security and Defense Policy Center, see http://www.rand.org/nsrd/ndri/centers/isdp.html or contact the director (contact information is provided on the web page).

Contents

Figures and Tables

Figures

Tables

Summary

The French-led military intervention in Mali that began on January 11, 2013, has succeeded in scattering, and severely weakening, the Islamist groups that had seized control of the northern half of the country over the course of the previous year. The French campaign brought most of the region back under at least nominal Malian government control. However, it has not addressed any of the political and ethnic conflicts that generated the crisis, and these conflicts are already reasserting themselves. Clashes between the Malian army and the Tuareg group that started the rebellion in early 2012, the National Movement for the Liberation of Azawad (Mouvement national de libération de l'Azawad [MNLA]), as well as the continuing insurgent and terrorist activities of the Movement for Unity and Jihad in West Africa (MUJWA) despite the continuing presence of French troops, bodes poorly for Bamako's ability to control the region in the future. It emphasizes the need to craft new political and security arrangements that will offer better prospects for stability. Figure S.1 shows Mali and its neighbors.

Although many Mali and peace-building experts speak of the need for greater political inclusion, foreign security assistance, and integration of northerners into Mali's armed forces and administration, their proposals are short on details. This report attempts to fill that gap and suggest a more efficient application of limited resources by (1) providing more-concrete information as to the viability of specific political and security arrangements, given Mali's past experience; (2) identifying the political actors that are most likely to play a role in the future political and security arrangements in northern Mali; and

Figure S.1
Map of Mali

SOURCE: Central Intelligence Agency, "Mali," last updated June 20, 2014a.

RAND *RR892-S.1*

(3) drawing on lessons learned from similar conflicts in the surrounding region—in particular, Niger.

Study Purpose and Approach

This report builds on recent RAND work on the communities and politics of northern Mali by identifying, with as much specificity as possible, the political and security arrangements that would offer the best prospects for enduring peace and stability, as well as the potential pitfalls that such arrangements might encounter and the actors most likely to help sustain those arrangements. This involves addressing the efficacy of some past conflict-mitigation mechanisms used in northern Mali—such as political agreements and integration of former militants into security forces—as well as identifying some of the individuals, institutions, and groups with the influence and legitimacy to make a significant contribution to a negotiated settlement. In the process, this report examines why past peace accords failed and the extent to which those failures can be attributed to poor implementation and lack of good will from Bamako (the most commonly heard explanation) or to the presence of "spoilers" among northern communities whose political interests clashed with other factions. The aim of this investigation is to provide informed recommendations for avoiding such failures and for forging an enduring peace. The methods used for this purpose have been to survey Malian media and to interview academics, local regional experts, and members of relevant Malian communities in Bamako to refine the data collected from other sources. Interviews focused on foreign and local actors experienced with past Malian peace accords or regional and local dynamics.

After an introduction in Chapter One, Chapter Two takes stock of northern Mali's past peace-accord implementation. In Chapter Three, we examine the five key challenges that have proved recurrent: the lack of representativeness of the peace-accord signatories, who represent only a small portion of the northern population; a flawed understanding of decentralization and democracy; Bamako's limited perceived legitimacy in the north; persistent insecurity; and an absence of transitional justice and reconciliation. Chapter Four examines how building representation through a variety of measures (e.g., improved democratic processes, political inclusion of traditional chiefs) can simultaneously address these five challenges and help craft a peaceful way forward for northern Mali. Chapter Five takes a more regional view of these challenges to explore whether Niger's relative stability during Mali's political and military crisis might be attributable to a "Nigerien model" of resilience and to draw potential lessons for Mali.

xii Achieving Peace in Northern Mali

Taking Stock of Mali's Rebellions and Peace-Accord Implementation

Mali's previous peace accords represent a useful place to begin assessing the problems that stand in the way of the emergence of a durable peace today. Between 1960 and the present, there have been four rebellions (1963 to 1964, 1990 to 1996, 2006 to 2009, and 2012 to 2013) that gave rise to four different peace accords:

- Accord sur la cessation des hostilités [Agreement on the cessation of hostilities, 1991, or the Tamanrasset Accord]
- Pacte national conclu entre le gouvernement de la République du Mali et les Mouvements et fronts unifiés de l'Azawad consacrant le statut particulier du Nord du Mali [National Pact between the government of the Republic of Mali and Unified Movements and Fronts of Azawad dedicating the special status of Northern Mali, 1992, or the National Pact]
- Accords d'Alger de 2006 [Algiers Accords of 2006]
- Accord préliminaire à l'élection présidentielle et aux pourparlers inclusifs de paix au Mali [Preliminary agreement for the presidential election and inclusive peace talks in Mali, 2013, or the Ouagadougou Accord].

Perhaps the most striking feature of the first three accords is their redundancy. They commit the Malian state to more or less the same things:

- the recognition of the north's special status
- the provision of a greater voice and role for the people of the north through decentralization
- better treatment by Bamako and its armed forces, who are required to lessen their presence and role
- the promotion of economic development in the north
- the integration of some rebel combatants into Mali's security forces and administration.

The Ouagadougou Accord has a different status because it focuses on the cease-fire, the preparation of the presidential election, the return of public services in the north, and the elaboration of a framework for broader and more-substantive future peace talks.

The 1963–1964 rebellion did not result in a peace accord because the Malian state put down the rebellion brutally and exacted retribution on Arabs and Tuareg. What it did was establish relations between the Malian government and the north on an antagonistic footing, leaving a legacy of lingering resentments. The 1992 National Pact resulted in the integration into the army and administration of close to 2,500 former combatants and the provision of financial subsidies to 9,500 more. These numbers were, however, perceived as too small in the north and too large, favoring the troublemakers, in the south. Disarmament was relatively unsuccessful in spite of the well-publicized Flame of Peace monument in Timbuktu that commemorates the burning of close to 3,000 weapons. Decentralization efforts were more successful; the number of communes (administrative units) increased from 19 to 703, and the first communal elections were held in 1998. A third region was created in northern Mali around Kidal.

Violence resumed in northern Mali in 2006 in ways that were highly reminiscent of the 1990s rebellion. The Algiers Accords negotiated under the mediation of Algeria granted northern Mali further political autonomy and more development funds. As in the 1990s, however, only a few of the accords' provisions were implemented. Four years later, president Amadou Toumani Touré (ATT) made a belated effort to improve both development and security in the north by means of a program known as the Special Program for Peace, Security, and Development in Northern Mali (Programme spécial pour la paix, la sécurité et le développement du Nord Mali, or PSPSDN), but the program was much criticized as poorly implemented and is even seen as one of the reasons that the MNLA took up arms in January 2012.

The repetitive nature of the accords and the grievances they reflect encourage the impression that nothing has changed since 1990, that the "northern problem" has not evolved, and that no progress has been made. Such an impression is incorrect in that the situation has evolved in important ways, and the past agreements have brought about certain accomplishments that, although they do not solve the root causes of unrest, have at least partially addressed some of them while generating a new set of conditions that need to be taken into consideration.

Explaining the Failure of Peace Accords

The peace accords did not bring about enduring peace for a variety of reasons. Bad faith and poor implementation are often cited as reasons for the accords' failure, and there is truth to both allegations. Of more interest are problems related to the narrow representativeness of the parties to the peace accords, the armed rebel movements. These groups, despite their claims to speak for the three northern regions, which they call Azawad, have never represented more than small minorities within minorities, leaving everyone else to regard themselves as not having been a party to the agreements. Just as importantly, the available evidence suggests that local politics and parochial interests have been at least as important motivators for rebellion as political grievances against Bamako, suggesting that, even if Bamako were fully to comply with the agreements, the agreements would not bring about peace.

Among the more-important gains of the peace accords were the decentralization and democratization movements initiated in 1992, with the goal of involving more of Mali's diverse population in governance. Although Malian and outside observers generally consider the gains associated with decentralization and democratization positive, closer inspection reveals a host of problems, ranging from poor implementation and an acute lack of resources to an immature political culture in which electoral competition is seen as a zero-sum game that exacerbates, rather than relieves, intercommunal tensions. Another problem is that the system established in the 1990s assigned no particular place to traditional chiefs, who, historically, have been among the locally accepted sources of decentralized authority. As a result, they have often found democracy threatening and have hindered Mali's democracy by trying to capture elected positions and blocking democratization.

Added to this is Bamako's fundamental failure to establish legitimacy among many northerners. Since independence, Bambara and other Mandé ethnicities have been at the core of Malian national identity, leaving Arabs and Tuareg feeling excluded. The integration of Arab and Tuareg fighters into Mali's armed forces, although good in principle, has been inadequately implemented.

Meanwhile, persistent insecurity reinforces the inclination to fall back on solidarity networks, such as clans, tribes, and ethnic groups, while undermining the legitimacy of the Malian army. This army is criticized both because it cannot provide security and because it should not, given its treatment of northerners. One conclusion is that the army needs to become more representative of the nation and seen less as a "foreign" force as much as it needs to improve its operational effectiveness.

Last, transitional justice and reconciliation are absent in Mali. Malians on all sides of the conflict complain of impunity, of no accountability for the crimes of individuals, groups, or the state, especially because armed group leaders, rather than being punished, have essentially been rewarded.

Moving Forward

The above analysis of the failings of the past peace accords suggests that emphasis needs to be given toward building representativeness, by, in effect, working around the unrepresentative armed groups to bring as many factions and communities into as large a tent as possible. Decentralization and democratization help, although these processes should be improved. Another recommendation would be to find ways to integrate traditional chiefs into government so that they can play constructive roles.

The question remains of what to do with the armed groups. They have to be negotiated with, but without being mistaken about the extent of their representativeness or the value of agreements with them. Ultimately, Bamako's objective should be to make them irrelevant by undertaking genuine efforts to implement the provisions of peace accords. Such reforms would give northerners a greater stake in supporting Malian unity rather than armed groups, whether secular or Islamists.

Is There a Nigerien Model of Resilience?

Niger's relative stability has made it a useful partner for U.S. and French counterterrorism cooperation efforts, as well as a platform for both nations' counterterrorism operations. Of interest is whether its stability can be attributed to any particular factors that could be emulated in Mali. One hypothesis is that Niger is structurally different: Demographics and geography—more specifically, greater ethnic integration and a less dramatic north–south divide—make Niger more resilient. Another is that Niger's policies toward returnees and northerners in general following the collapse of Libya were more beneficial than Bamako's inaction in this regard.

Finally, a third hypothesis is that Niger might have simply been lucky so far, and its more-favorable structural conditions and policies might not be sufficient in the future considering the long-standing and emerging threats that the country is facing, as well as its history of past political instability.

Notwithstanding our ambivalence about Niger's ability to remain stable in the near future, we recommend emulating some of the policies that could account for the progress made so far, such as better integration of Tuareg populations and a focus on development programs in addition to security.

Conclusion and Recommendations

The peace accords of the past have not promoted peace and national unity, but it cannot be said that no progress has been made or that Mali is precisely back to where it started. The situation has evolved considerably, and there are clear indications about what has worked and what Mali should pursue. The government should prioritize improvements to the system created by the National Pact of the 1990s—namely, the integration of the Malian army and greater decentralization and democracy.

Ultimately, what Mali has been lacking is representativeness, compounded by the fact that the rebel groups that profess to speak for everyone actually speak for very few. Those few should not be ignored, but Bamako's focus needs to be on including everyone else in the country's polity and key institutions.

This relates to the question of security, the inefficacy of Mali's armed forces, and their tendency to alienate northerners. Focus must be given to the question of how Mali's army can be changed so that northerners no longer regard it as an "occupying force." Another focus should be on helping Mali's government become more legitimate in the eyes of northerners. The idea of bringing traditional chiefs on board to involve them is intriguing and merits further consideration. Similarly, the chiefs and other community leaders might well hold the key for local contributions to maintaining security.

Niger also offers important lessons with respect to alternative government policies, approaches to integrating Tuareg in government, and the value of development-focused policies.

Finally, it should also be clear that there is no quick fix for Mali. Mali's terrorism problem is nested within a larger security problem, which is, in turn, nested within several other problems, ranging from economic constraints to governance.

Acknowledgments

We are grateful for the support of many individuals over the course of this research project. First, we would like to express our sincere thanks for the support from our study sponsors, LTC Gabriel Chinchilla, Mark Swayne, and Pauline Kusiak, who provided us with helpful guidance and comments throughout this project. This research would not have been possible without people sharing with us their expertise regarding Malian and Nigerien politics and society. We are particularly thankful to those community leaders and other individuals who met with Michael Shurkin in Bamako in October 2013, providing invaluable input to our research. We also thank the U.S. and foreign researchers who took the time to speak with us during this project.

Additional thanks go to Alexis Arieff, Pierre Boilley, Emmanuel Grégoire, Charles Grémont, Farley Mesko, Peter Tinti, Susanna Wing, and Eric Wulf for their support and insights. We are grateful to Andrew Goodhart and Julie Taylor for the initial impulse they gave to this project. Likewise, our efforts in Mali would have been fruitless had it not been for the help of Aminatou Ansari, Ahmed Ag Abdoulaye, and Chris Runyan.

We also thank our reviewers, Alexis Arieff and Larry Hanauer, for their helpful comments on an earlier draft of this report.

Finally, our thanks go to Beth Bernstein, Lisa Bernard, and Ilana Blum for their editing support. Any errors are solely our responsibility.

Abbreviations

ADC	Democratic Alliance of 23 May for Change (Alliance démocratique du 23 mai 2006 pour le changement)
AFISMA	African-Led International Support Mission in Mali
AQIM	al Qaeda in the Islamic Maghreb
ARLA	Revolutionary Liberation Army of Azawad (Armée révolutionnaire de libération de l'Azawad)
ATNM	Alliance Touareg Niger–Mali
ATT	Amadou Toumani Touré
FAN	Nigerien Armed Forces (Forces armées nigériennes)
FIAA	Arabic Islamic Front of Azawad (Front islamique arabe de l'Azawad)
FLAA	Air and Azawak Liberation Front (Front de libération de l'Aïr et de l'Azawak)
FNLA	National Liberation Front of Azawad (Front de libération nationale de l'Azawad)
FPLA	Popular Liberation Front of Azawad (Front populaire de libération de l'Azawad)

FPR	Patriotic Resistance Forces (Forces patriotiques de résistance)
HCUA	Haut conseil pour l'unité de l'Azawad
MAA	Arab Movement of Azawad (Mouvement arabe de l'Azawad)
MFUA	Unified Azawad Movements and Fronts (Mouvements et fronts unifiés de l'Azawad)
MIA	Mouvement islamique de l'Azawad
MINUSMA	United Nations Multidimensional Integrated Stabilization Mission in Mali
MNA	National Movement of Azawad (Mouvement national de l'Azawad)
MNJ	Niger Movement for Justice (Mouvement des Nigériens pour la justice)
MNLA	National Movement for the Liberation of Azawad (Mouvement national de libération de l'Azawad)
MPA	Popular Movement of Azawad (Mouvement populaire de l'Azawad)
MPLA	Popular Movement for the Liberation of Azawad (Mouvement populaire pour la libération de l'Azawad)
MUJWA	Movement for Unity and Jihad in West Africa
PDES	Plan de développement économique et social
PSPSDN	Special Program for Peace, Security, and Development in Northern Mali (Programme spécial pour la paix, la sécurité et le développement du Nord Mali)
SDS	Strategy for Development and Security

UFRA	Union of the Forces of Armed Resistance (Union des forces de la résistance armée)
UN	United Nations
UNDP	United Nations Development Programme

CHAPTER ONE

Introduction

I am persuaded that Mali can no longer be like before.
—Bellah community leader[1]

In the aftermath of Mali's annus horribilis of 2012 and its rescue by France in January 2013, Mali's friends and partners are interested in ensuring that, *this* time, peace and stability will endure. This interest is particularly keen given the newfound recognition that Mali's terrorism problem—which is a key driver of U.S. and French involvement—cannot be addressed on a long-term basis without addressing Mali's broader political and security challenges.

The challenge of ensuring peace in northern Mali is daunting for a variety of reasons. First, it has been tried before. Since 1991, the year Mali returned to civilian rule, the government has signed four peace accords with Tuareg and Arab armed groups. (See Figure 1.1 for a map of the region.) Second, in the mid-1990s, Mali began a major effort to decentralize and democratize the country by standing up numerous subnational administrations, run, in many cases, by elected officials. On paper at least, northern Malians have as much opportunity to participate in regional and national political processes as any other Malians have and thus cannot credibly claim to be disenfranchised. Northerners from many different communities, for example, ran in legislative elections and were elected to sit in the National Assembly in Bamako. Third, instability and insecurity have persisted, even though

---

[1] Bellah leader, interview with Michael Shurkin, Bamako, October 8, 2013.

Figure 1.1
Map of Mali

SOURCE: Central Intelligence Agency, "Mali," last updated June 20, 2014a.
RAND *RR892-1.1*

many former combatants from northern rebel groups were integrated into the Malian armed forces. These three dynamics have led many observers to see Mali's problems as intractable.

Although the repetition of the conflict/peace accord cycle in Mali might seem disheartening, it also offers valuable lessons on what peace-building measures have worked or not over time. In other words, a historical examination of Mali's past peace accords and how they were implemented can provide insights into what might be needed for the current peace talks to finally bring lasting stability to Mali.

This report examines the content and results of northern Mali's peace settlements since the early 1990s to identify flaws and successes. Looking at these past agreements in the context of the problems Mali faces today, this report identifies five recurrent issues: the lack of representativeness of the peace-accord signatories, who represent little more than small minorities within minorities; a flawed understanding of decentralization and democracy; Bamako's limited perceived legitimacy in the north; persistent insecurity; and an absence of transitional justice and reconciliation. This report further discusses how building representativeness (through improved democratic processes, political inclusion of traditional chiefs, and skillful handling of armed groups) can address all five issues simultaneously and help craft a peaceful way forward for Mali. A final section in this report takes a more regional view to examine how Mali's neighbor Niger, although faced with similar challenges, succeeded in remaining at peace. That section explores whether Niger owes its survival to a more favorable context, shrewd policies, or sheer luck and whether it could offer a model of resilience for northern Mali.

The methods used for this study have been to survey Malian media and the literature pertaining to northern Malian political and societal dynamics. Because of the paucity of published resources in that area, however, interviews with local regional experts, academics, and members of relevant Malian communities in Bamako have been essential to refining the data collected from other sources. Interviews focused on foreign and local actors experienced with past Malian peace accords or regional and local dynamics.

Clearly, northern Mali is not all of Mali, and there are many more institutional issues to solve in Mali than the ones pertaining to the administration and stability of the regions of Kidal, Gao, and Timbuktu. It is also important to remember that Arabs and Tuareg, whose dynamics this report focuses on, represent minorities in a country that is majority-populated by Bambara, a sedentary ethnic group. Considering how disruptive political turmoil in the north has been since the country's independence from France, however, addressing these issues would go a long way in providing Bamako with the environment it needs to strengthen its institutions and in preventing the future resurgence of a scenario similar to the one that played out in 2012–2013 and led to the quasi-collapse of the Malian state and the deployment of French and African troops in the country.

CHAPTER TWO

A Brief History of Mali's Rebellions and the Implementation of Peace Accords

Mali's previous peace accords represent a useful place to begin assessing the problems that stand in the way of the emergence of a durable peace today. Between 1960 and the present, Mali has experienced four rebellions (1963 to 1964, 1990 to 1996, 2006 to 2009, and 2012 to 2013) that gave rise to four different peace accords outlined in Table 2.1.

The Ouagadougou Accord differs from the first three in the sense that, as it title states, it is a "preliminary" agreement whose focus is limited to short-term issues

- a cease-fire
- the preparation of the presidential election
- the return of public services in the north
- the elaboration of a framework for broader and more-substantive future peace talks.[1]

As of early 2015, this more comprehensive peace agreement was not yet in sight.

Two striking features characterize the 1991, 1992, and 2006 peace accords. One is the fact that each is with a different armed group,

---

[1] Accord préliminaire à l'élection présidentielle et aux pourparlers inclusifs de paix au Mali [Preliminary agreement for the presidential election and inclusive peace talks in Mali], Ouagadougou, Burkina Faso, June 18, 2013.

Table 2.1
Peace Accords Signed in Mali Since Independence

Date	Full Name	Short Name	Signatories
January 6, 1991	Accord sur la cessation des hostilités: Le gouvernement de la République du Mali d'une part et le Mouvement Populaire de l'Azaouad et le Front Islamique Arabe d'autre part [Agreement on the cessation of hostilities: The government of the Republic of Mali on the one hand and the MPA and the FIAA on the other]	Tamanrasset Accord	Government of the Republic of Mali MPA FIAA
April 11, 1992	Pacte national conclu entre le gouvernement de la République du Mali et les Mouvements et fronts unifiés de l'Azawad consacrant le statut particulier du nord du Mali [National Pact between the government of the Republic of Mali and the MFUA dedicating the special status of northern Mali]	National Pact	Government of the Republic of Mali MFUA
July 4, 2006	Accords d'Alger de 2006: Restauration de la paix, de la sécurité et du développement dans la région de Kidal [Algiers Accords of 2006: Restoration of peace, security, and development in the region of Kidal]	Algiers Accords	Government of the Republic of Mali ADC
June 18, 2013	Accord préliminaire à l'élection présidentielle et aux pourparlers inclusifs de paix au Mali [Preliminary agreement for the presidential election and inclusive peace talks in Mali]	Ouagadougou Accord	Government of the Republic of Mali MNLA HCUA

NOTE: Because they did not involve the state of Mali, we exclude the Bourem accords from the table. The Ganda Koy (the main Songhai combatant group) and the Popular Liberation Front of Azawad (Front populaire de libération de l'Azawad [FPLA]) signed these accords in January 1995. MPA = Mouvement populaire de l'Azawad. FIAA = Arab Islamic Front of Azawad (Front islamique Arabe de l'Azawad). MFUA = Unified Azawad Movements and Fronts (Mouvements et fronts unifiés de l'Awazad). ADC = May 23 Democratic Alliance for Change (Alliance démocratique du 23 mai 2006 pour le changement). MNLA = Mouvement national de libération de l'Azawad. HCUA = Haut conseil pour l'unité de l'Azawad.

a problem that we discuss below. The other is the accords' redundancy. They commit the Malian state to more or less the same things:

- the recognition of the north's special status
- the provision of a greater voice and role for the people of the north through decentralization
- better treatment by Bamako and its armed forces, who are required to lessen their presence and role
- the promotion of economic development in the north
- the integration of some rebel combatants into Mali's security forces and administration.

The repetitive nature of the accords and the grievances they reflect encourage the impression that nothing has changed since 1990, that the "northern problem" has not evolved, and that no progress has been made. Such an impression is incorrect in that the situation has evolved in important ways, and the past agreements have brought about certain accomplishments that, although they do not solve the basic problems that have prompted unrest, have at least partially addressed some of them while generating a new set of conditions that need to be taken into consideration. There is now, moreover, a track record that gives some indication of what works and what does not. In order to explore the changes that have taken place, it is useful to review some of the basics of northern Mali's population, the events of the past decades, and the details of the three peace accords that preceded the most recent one signed in Ouagadougou in June 2013.

A Diverse and Divided Population

Mali's division between north and south is best understood as a porous boundary between two climates (desert in the north and subtropical in the south, with the Sahelian belt in the middle) and two broad patterns of populations.[2] In the south, where roughly 90 percent of Mali's population lives, the largest group is the Bambara, who also dominate Mali's government and military and who ruled southern Mali for much of the past centuries. The northern regions are Gao, Timbuktu, and Kidal. Timbuktu and Gao are located in the ethnically diverse region of the Niger River bend, which includes numerous farming and fishing communities populated by an array of settled and semi-nomadic ethnic groups—most prominently the Songhais and Peuls. Farther north, beyond the Niger River is mostly desertic with few urban centers, the most important being Kidal. Arabs and Tuareg straddle both areas, with the Tuareg presence extending north and east to Algeria, Niger, and Libya.

Mali's population groups are divided internally. Tuareg are organized into confederations divided by caste and clan and both horizontal and vertical hierarchies.[3] Each confederation consists of numerous clusters of noble clans, with each cluster associated with clusters of subordinate clans, as well as artisan clans and former-slave clans (see Figure 2.1). At the top of the system is a (usually elected) chief known as an *amenokal*. The dominant Tuareg confederation since the beginning of the 20th century has been the Kel Adagh confederation, and the dominant noble clans within that confederation are known as Ifoghas. The French are largely responsible for the Kel Adagh dominance, having allied with the Kel Adagh during the colonization period to combat the Kel Adagh's more powerful competitor, the Iwellemmedan confederation. The French then used the support of the Kel Adagh to secure the region against cross-border raiders.[4]

---

[2]   This section draws largely from Stephanie Pezard and Michael Shurkin, *Toward a Secure and Stable Mali: Approaches to Engaging Local Actors*, Santa Monica, Calif.: RAND Corporation, RR-296-OSD, 2013.

[3]   *Clan* is the term most commonly used for Tuareg groupings, whereas *tribe* is the term applied to Arabs.

[4]   For a general discussion of the Iwellemmedan, see Charles Grémont, *Les Touaregs Iwellemedan (1647–1896): Un ensemble politique de la Boucle du Niger*, Paris: Karthala, 2010a; Charles Grémont, *Touaregs et Arabes dans les forces armées coloniales et maliennes: Une histoire en trompe-l'œil*, Paris: Institut français des relations internationales, 2010b; and Pierre Boilley, *Les Touaregs Kel Adagh: Dépendances et révoltes—du Soudan français au Mali contem-*

Similar divisions straddle Arab communities, which historically have had their own confederations, complete with noble and vassal clans, warrior elites, and religious elites. The two major Arab confederations are the Berabiche and the Kuntas. Mali's Songhai communities have a more horizontal organization: They are organized by villages in which elders elect village chiefs.[5] In contrast, Peul society traditionally has been at least as stratified as Tuareg society.

First Tuareg Rebellion: 1963–1964

Soon after Mali became independent in 1960, a combination of factors induced a portion of the Kidal-centered Kel Adagh Tuareg confederation to take up arms against the new government. Bamako had applied economic and other policies inimical to Tuareg in general in favor of communities that traditionally had been subordinate to Tuareg or Tuareg nobles. According to Mali expert Jean Sebastian Lecocq, "the administration set out to forcibly alter Tamasheq [Tuareg] society," largely through attempts to alter its economic profile, make it sedentary, and overturn its social hierarchies.[6] Although Lecocq notes that, by and large, Bamako's policies were ineffective and changed little on the ground, they antagonized nomadic populations. They also constituted a reversal of French colonial policies, which had frozen certain aspects of northern Mali's social hierarchy. In particular, the lead clans of the Kel Adagh—whom France helped establish and maintain supremacy atop the hierarchy—hoped that the new independent government of Mali would negotiate a similar arrangement with them that

---

porain, Paris: Éd. Karthala, 1999, provide further details of the French relationship with the Kel Adagh and the overthrow of the Iwellemmedan.

[5]   Ronald Wesley Niezen, *Diverse Styles of Islamic Reform Among the Songhay of Eastern Mali*, Cambridge, UK: Cambridge University, thesis, October 27, 1987, pp. 37–38.

[6]   Jean Sebastian Lecocq, *That Desert Is Our Country: Tuareg Rebellions and Competing Nationalisms in Contemporary Mali (1946–1996)*, Amsterdam: Universiteit von Amsterdam, doctoral thesis, 2002, p. 97.

Figure 2.1
The Structure and Hierarchies of the Kel Adagh Confederation

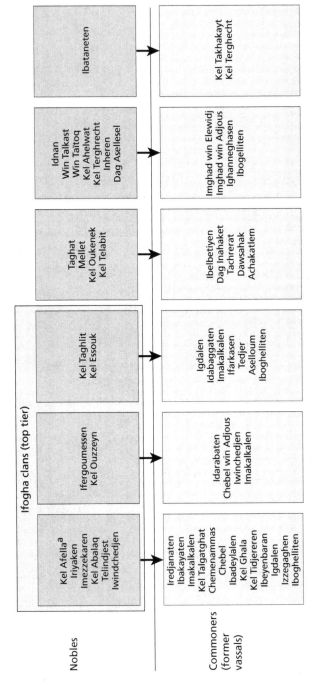

SOURCE: Boilley, 1999, p. 47.

NOTE: Arrows refer to traditional relationships of dependence.

[a] The traditional leader of the Kel Adagh, the amenokal, is Kel Afella.

RAND RR892-2.1

recognized their status.[7] They were disappointed, and it is therefore not an accident that they and not other clans took up arms against Bamako.

This initial Tuareg rebellion against the Malian central power highlights an important fact that would prove true again in every subsequent political crisis: Not all Tuareg get involved in, or even support, taking up arms. Far from being a generalized, popular revolt, the 1963 rebellion was the work of a few "noble" (i.e., upper-caste) leaders of certain elite clans atop the Kel Adagh confederation.[8]

Non-Tuareg did not participate, nor did Mali's other large Tuareg confederations.[9] It should also be noted that only a portion of the clans involved in the rebellion took up arms, and the amenokal himself opposed the conflict, although, at the time, he disputed the position with his brother, who was among the rebellion's leaders.[10] To say that a particular clan was involved does not indicate the entire clan or even most of its members, but rather some portion.

Because the Malian state put down the rebellion brutally and exacted retribution on Arabs and Tuareg, notwithstanding the fact that none of the former and few of the latter had been involved, the 1963–1964 rebellion did not result in a peace accord.[11] What it did was establish relations between the Malian government and the north on an antagonistic footing, leaving a legacy of lingering resentment.

---

[7] Lecocq, 2002, p. 124.

[8] More specifically the Kel Afella—the clan of the Kel Adagh amenokal—along with the Iriyaken, Idnan, Irregenaten, Ifergoumessen, and Taghat Mellet clans, who were able to mobilize some of their subordinate "commoner" clans (Boilley, 1999, pp. 334–335).

[9] The Kel Antsar and the Kel Iwellemmedan (Boilley, 1999, p. 334).

[10] Boilley, 1999, p. 335.

[11] Lecocq argues that the rebellion's leaders never expected to win. Their goal, according to Lecocq, was to attract international intention and provoke intervention on their behalf by Algeria or France, and they expected Algeria to arbitrate between them and Mali. See Jean Sebastian Lecocq, *Disputed Desert: Decolonisation, Competing Nationalism and Tuareg Rebellions in Northern Mali*, Leiden: Brill, 2010, p. 135.

Second Tuareg Rebellion: 1990–1996

The decades that followed the first rebellion were not kind to northern Mali, which, in addition to suffering from state policies that systematically favored the southern regions, was battered by successive droughts that badly eroded the region's economy and, in particular, the ability of nomadic Tuareg populations to sustain themselves. Many moved to Bamako and other points south, ended up in aid camps, or left the country in search of work. Of the latter, a significant portion went to Libya, where some enrolled in Muammar Qadhafi's Islamic Legion and served in wars in Chad and Lebanon. Exile and military service had a radicalizing effect, giving many northerners a new identity as Malian Tuareg that, for some, was accompanied by a desire to transcend northern Mali's traditional hierarchies. Young returning Libyan army veterans formed the core of the movement that, on June 28, 1990, attacked a military outpost in Ménaka, setting off Mali's second Tuareg rebellion. Their leader was Iyad Ag Ghaly, a Libyan army combat veteran and member of the noble Kel Adagh clan, the Iriyaken.

As had been the case in the past, a few elite Kel Adagh clans, most notably the Iriyaken, were in the forefront of events and provided most of the movement's leadership. However, French Tuareg expert Pierre Boilley stresses that, at least initially, there was no indication of a clan- or caste-centered agenda. On the contrary, the militants seemed to share the new spirit of pan-Tuareg unity.[12] Indeed, the demands of Ag Ghaly's group, the Popular Movement for the Liberation of Azawad (Mouvement populaire pour la libération de l'Azawad [MPLA]), ostensibly reflected the interests of the entire community. They included a reduced Malian army presence in the north, more political power for local actors, and more resources for development projects in the north. Unlike in 1963, this time, a broad array of Tuareg communities—most notably nonnoble and non–Kel Adagh clans—and Arab communities joined the fight, with the Arabs forming their own rebel group, the FIAA. Bamako responded with state repression, although, this time,

---

12 Boilley, 1999, p. 481.

the rebels, thanks in part to their Libyan training, did considerably better in fighting back the Malian army.

President Moussa Traoré eventually agreed to enter into negotiations with the rebel leaders in Tamanrasset, Algeria, resulting in the signing on January 6, 1991, of a peace accord between Bamako, the MPA (what was formerly the MPLA), and the FIAA. The Tamanrasset accord granted the north special status, with more political and administrative power given to local populations. It also provided for a lesser presence of the army in the north; the demilitarization of administration; the dismantling of several military posts; military withdrawal from grazing areas, as well as densely populated areas; and the granting of close to 50 percent of an upcoming development program to northern regions.[13] At the time, the content of this accord was not publicly divulged for fear that the south would perceive it as unacceptable.[14]

This accord was never implemented. Two months after its signing, Traoré was ousted in a coup, and Lieutenant Colonel Amadou Toumani Touré (ATT) replaced him at the head of a transitional government. Meanwhile, in the north, Tuareg unity quickly fragmented along clan and caste lines. "In the end," Lecocq observed, "who you are and who your family is, remained more important [than] the ideal of . . . the Kel Tamasheq nation."[15] The MPA shook out to become the militia of the elite Kel Adagh aristocratic clans, including the amenokal's Kel Afella, Iyad Ag Ghaly's Iriyaken, and the Ifergoumessen. The FPLA gathered a variety of other clans to its ranks but ultimately was dominated by the Chemenammas, a commoner clan on the periphery of the Kel Adagh confederation.[16] It eventually broke into smaller fac-

---

[13] Accord sur la cessation des hostilités: Le gouvernement de la République du Mali d'une part et le Mouvement Populaire de l'Azaouad et le Front Islamique Arabe d'autre part [Agreement on the cessation of hostilities: The government of the Republic of Mali on the one hand and the Popular Movement Azaouad and the Arab Islamic Front on the other], Tamanrasset, Algeria, January 6, 1991.

[14] Mériadec Raffray, "Les rébellions touarègues au Sahel," French Ministry of Defense, July 1, 2013, p. 60.

[15] Lecocq, 2002, p. 268.

[16] Lecocq, 2002, p. 267.

tions, each aligned with specific clans, some associated with the Kel Adagh and some with other confederations—most notably, the Kel Ouillimiden.[17] Lastly, there was the Revolutionary Liberation Army of Azawad (Armée révolutionnaire de libération de l'Azawad [ARLA]), a commoner-based group keen on overthrowing the traditional Tuareg hierarchies.[18]

It took pressure from Algeria to bring all Tuareg and Arab rebel groups into a single coalition, the MFUA, which eventually started negotiations with the ATT-led transitional government.[19] On April 11, 1992, they eventually signed a new text known as the National Pact, which provided largely the same concessions as the Tamanrasset Accord—in particular, a special status for the north, mentioned in the full title of the document—with additional details on the modalities of transfers of power to locals and the integration of rebels into the Malian administration and army. It reorganized the administrative divisions of all of Mali, so that populations in the southern half of the country would also benefit from the new decentralization measures. It also created a new region, Kidal, giving its residents greater political clout despite making up a tiny population. Bamako would transfer some of its prerogatives to newly created regional and local assemblies. Bamako also agreed to reduce its military presence in the north and to funnel more funds for development programs toward the north. The position of commissary for the north would be created to oversee implementation of the National Pact for the coming five years.[20]

In spite of the National Pact, the north remained at war. Rebel and militia groups continued fighting each other and the Malian army.

---

[17] Lecocq, 2002, p. 267.

[18] Boilley, 1999, pp. 505–510.

[19] Modibo Keita, *La résolution du conflit touareg au Mali et au Niger*, Groupe de recherche sur les interventions de paix dans les conflits intra-étatiques, Note de recherche 10, July 2002, p. 17.

[20] Pacte national conclu entre le gouvernement de la République du Mali et les Mouvements et fronts unifiés de l'Azawad consacrant le statut particulier du Nord du Mali [National Pact between the government of the Republic of Mali and the Unified Movements and Fronts of Azawad dedicating the special status of northern Mali], Bamako, April 11, 1992.

Part of the problem, according to Lecocq, was that many northerners saw the creation of a Kidal region as evidence that the Malian state was following the lead of the French colonial authorities in granting particular privileges to the Kel Adagh.[21] Tuareg and rebel groups started fighting each other, while another component of the northern Malian population, the sedentary Songhai in the Gao region, set up their own militias, the Ganda Koy.[22] Soon, the violence started targeting civilians on both sides. The implementation of the National Pact hence started against a less-than-favorable backdrop. In February 1993, 640 former rebels were integrated in the Malian army, while 13 high-ranking MFUA officials became technical advisers in various ministries.[23] When violence finally receded in 1996, the integration of former combatants picked up speed to reach 2,490 combatants integrated into the army or the administration that year. About 9,500 more received financial support to reintegrate into economic life by starting, for instance, small businesses.[24] These reintegration efforts were relatively successful. By 2000, 90 percent of those former combatants were still in the army or the new civilian jobs they had secured through the reintegration process.[25] However, Mali expert Susanna Wing notes that, even though close to 1,500 Tuareg were integrated into the Malian army and administration, "this was a small number relative to the entire Tuareg population and tended to promote certain groups within the Tuareg—Kel Antsar and Imghad in particular."[26] Non-Tuareg also saw Tuareg integration as favoritism, creating resentment.[27] Meanwhile, disarmament proved only mildly successful. In spite of efforts to collect

---

[21] Lecocq, 2002, p. 270.

[22] *Ganda koy* means "masters of the land" in Songhai.

[23] Keita, 2002, p. 21.

[24] Keita, 2002, p. 23.

[25] Sophie Boukhari, "Mali: A Flickering Flame," *UNESCO Courier*, Vol. 53, No. 1, January 2000, pp. 26–28, p. 27.

[26] Susanna D. Wing, *Mali's Precarious Democracy and the Causes of Conflict*, Washington, D.C.: United States Institute of Peace, April 19, 2013, pp. 4–5.

[27] Wing, 2013, pp. 4–5.

them, weapons remained in large numbers in the hands of demobilized individuals and the general population.[28]

Decentralization efforts were more successful, at least in creating new administrative structures. The number of communes went from 19 to 703.[29] The first communal elections were held in urban municipalities in 1998 and in the nearly 700 rural communes in 1999.[30]

Third Tuareg Rebellion: 2006–2009

Violence resumed in northern Mali in 2006 in ways that were highly reminiscent of the 1990s rebellion. The rebellion started when 150 Tuareg officers from the Kidal region deserted their military barracks in Kidal, Ménaka, and Tessalit with weapons and army vehicles under the leadership of Hassan Ag Fagaga, a deserted Tuareg lieutenant colonel in the Malian army.[31] Iyad Ag Ghaly soon took over leadership of the new group, the ADC, and demanded the full implementation of the 1992 National Pact—in particular, more autonomy for northern regions, a special status for Kidal, and a more equitable distribution of national resources to foster development in the north.

To an important extent, the 2006 rebellion can be reduced to a bid by some upstart members of a Kel Adagh clan, the Ifergoumessen, to elevate their position relative to other clans. In the 1990s, the Ifergoumessen were with the MPA and thus had participated in that group's victory over Gamou's Imghad militia. Lecocq has argued that the genesis of the 2006 rebellion was Gamou's promotion and appointment to the position of commander of the Gao garrison over Colonel

---

[28] Nicolas Florquin and Stephanie Pezard, "Insurgency, Disarmament, and Insecurity in Northern Mali, 1990–2004," in Nicolas Florquin and Eric G. Berman, eds., *Armed and Aimless: Armed Groups, Guns, and Human Security in the ECOWAS Region*, Geneva: Small Arms Survey, May 2005, pp. 46–77, p. 68.

[29] Susanna D. Wing and Bréhima Kassibo, "Mali: Incentives and Challenges for Decentralization," in James Tyler Dickovick and James S. Wunsch, eds., *Decentralization in Africa: The Paradox of State Strength*, Boulder, Colo.: Lynne Rienner Publishers, 2014, pp. 184, 188.

[30] Wing and Kassibo, 2014, p. 188.

[31] Grémont, 2010b, p. 19; Lecocq, 2010, p. 391.

Hassan Fagaga, an Ifergoumessen and former MPA member who did not appreciate the rise of his erstwhile rivals. Fagaga deserted from the army and started the rebellion.[32] The ADC was, by all accounts, largely an Ifergoumessen affair, although not exclusively: The group attracted some Idnan fighters, and its nominal leader, Iyad, was an Iriyaken. Beyond these, all the available evidence suggests that the new rebellion attracted markedly little support from other northern groups.[33]

Bamako entered negotiations almost immediately with the ADC and signed a peace agreement within three months, the Algiers Accords, under the mediation of Algeria (which has, like Mali, a vested interested in containing Tuareg unrest, having a sizable Tuareg population itself). These accords specifically addressed issues in the region of Kidal, as underlined in their full title, but most provisions are largely similar to what had been promised in the Tamanrasset Accord and the National Pact. The accords created a regional assembly to be consulted on new laws affecting the Kidal region. The ADC obtained several concessions from the government in terms of economic and social development, including the organization of a forum with international donors to be held in Kidal; the implementation of a health system adapted to the nomadic way of life; new or improved infrastructures (building of an airport in Kidal, extension of electricity and phone networks, tarring of the roads from Kidal to Gao, Ménaka, and Algeria); and the renewal of the ten-year preferential tax regime meant to stimulate economic development that had been part of the National Pact but never implemented.[34] The combatants who had deserted were allowed back into the Malian army, which would largely retreat from the northern regions.

Under the agreement, security in the north would be implemented by security special units constituted mainly of northerners to be put in charge of basic security and patrolling missions. These new

---

[32] Lecocq, 2010, pp. 391, 400.

[33] Lecocq, 2010, p. 392.

[34] Accords d'Alger de 2006: Restauration de la paix, de la sécurité et du développement dans la région de Kidal [Algiers Accords of 2006: Restoration of peace, security, and development in the region of Kidal], July 4, 2006.

units were expected to have three benefits: They would provide former combatants with a legitimate occupation; reduce the army's footprint in an area where it was not welcomed; and reduce the army desertion rates that were due, in part, to the reluctance of northerners to be deployed in the south and to their feeling of being discriminated against by their largely non-Tuareg commanders. These units were to be placed under the authority of local military commanders to act in coordination with national security forces. Algeria not only played a key role in facilitating negotiations between Bamako and the Tuareg movements (as it had done already in the 1990s) but also played a part in the implementation of the Algiers Accords by being a participant in the accord's follow-up committee.

A minority of the participants in the 2006 uprising—led again by Fagaga, this time with Ibrahim Ag Bahanga—rejected the Algiers Accords and took up arms again less than a year later, in May 2007, this time as allies of a Nigerien Tuareg rebel movement.[35] Although the Malians participated in some fighting in Niger, the alliance was short lived, with the Malians once again concentrating on their own region under the flag of the Alliance Touareg Niger–Mali (ATNM). President ATT initially attempted to deal with them through negotiation until April and May 2008, when Bahanga launched an offensive that killed 63 Malian soldiers and struck as far south as the army base in Diabaly. Bamako then switched to a military option and enrolled the support of local Tuareg and Arab militias controlled by two officers of the Malian army—Tuareg Lieutenant Colonel El Haji Ag Gamou and Arab Colonel Mohammed Ould Meydou. By January 2009, Bahanga's ATNM had been decisively defeated. This second phase of the 2006 rebellion did not lead to a separate peace agreement, and the focus remained on implementing the 2006 Algiers Accords.

As in the 1990s, only a few of the accords' provisions were implemented. Bamako organized the Kidal Forum, which gathered all international donors to find financial support for a ten-year development plan for the Timbuktu, Gao, and Kidal regions. No clear timeline, however, was established for the realization of the numerous projects

---

[35] Lecocq, 2010, pp. 398–399.

that were outlined during the forum, beyond a 2016 target end date.[36] This forum was negatively perceived in southern Mali, which judged as unfair the attention that the north was getting.[37]

The Malian government conducted a disarmament, demobilization, and reintegration program with 600 former combatants who handed in their weapons in March 2007, with approximately 600 doing so in February 2009. Another measure targeted the militia of young Tuareg and Arabs who joined the military surge against the ATNM in early 2009. They were included in the socioeconomic reinsertion program for young ex-combatants and unemployed people set up by the Algiers Accords. Interestingly, the program targeted both categories so as not to seem to reward only the rebellion.

However, Bamako never set up the local, regional, and interregional assemblies that were supposed to be established in the north. The special security units and other security provisions never materialized. The implementation of economic efforts was disappointing as well. For example, the special investment fund called for by the Algiers Accords was never created.[38]

Four years later, in July 2010, ATT made a belated effort to improve both development and security in the north by means of a program known as the Special Program for Peace, Security, and Development in Northern Mali (Programme spécial pour la paix, la sécurité et le développement du Nord Mali [PSPSDN]). An ambitious program in scope and funding (about $60 million provided by several donors, including France, Canada, and the European Union), the PSPSDN was to focus development efforts on 11 strategic sites in northern Mali that would at the same time be secured by the Malian army.[39] It was,

---

[36] "ATT à la clôture du forum de Kidal," March 27, 2007.

[37] Raffray, 2013, p. 65.

[38] Wing, 2013, p. 6.

[39] Kalilou Sidibé, *Security Management in Northern Mali: Criminal Networks and Conflict Resolution Mechanisms*, Brighton, UK: Institute of Development Studies, Research Report 77, August 2012; International Crisis Group, *Mali: Éviter l'escalade*, Brussels, Africa Report 189, July 18, 2012, p. 7. For more details on the PSPSDN, see, for instance, Abdou-

however, criticized for being "too little, too late,"[40] for bringing back the Malian army in areas where it was not welcome, and for not consulting sufficiently with local populations.[41] The concept of building military barracks in the north on the strategic sites went directly against the efforts of the preceding 20 years to reduce the presence of the Malian army in the north and was criticized by Tuareg leaders as focusing more on security than on development, while being woefully inefficient against criminality.[42] Overall, while international donors were providing funds for the PSPSDN in the hope that it would finally implement some of the promises made in the Algiers Accords, the program apparently antagonized local populations and is even seen as one of the reasons that the MNLA took up arms in January 2012: Five months prior, the National Movement of Azawad (Mouvement national de l'Azawad [MNA]) had published a statement opposing the PSPSDN, which it claimed was militarizing the north rather than developing it, and called for international donors to halt their aid, which "will have no positive result but rather regrettable consequences for both sides."[43]

---

laye Niangaly, "Lancement officiel du PSPSDN: Enfin le bout du tunnel pour le Nord du Mali," *Le Prétoire* (Bamako), August 11, 2011.

[40] Berabiche leader, interview with Michael Shurkin, Bamako, October 4, 2013.

[41] Wing, 2013, pp. 7–8; Berabiche leader, 2013; Arab leader A, interview with Michael Shurkin, Bamako, October 11, 2013.

[42] International Crisis Group, 2012, p. 7.

[43] Mouvement National de l'Azawad, "Le Mouvement national de l'Azawad condamne le PSPSDN," *Journal du Mali*, September 4, 2011; see also International Crisis Group, 2012, p. 7.

In October 2011, the MNA merged with the ATNM (the same group that had conducted the 2007–2009 rebellion) and formed the MNLA.

The northern populations' perceptions of the Malian army are often ambiguous. The memory of the abuses against civilians committed in the 1990s is still present. The army, however, also represents an opportunity for those former combatants who want to be integrated into the Malian forces. It also represents a modicum of security against at least some security threats: As Hannah Armstrong describes, "demilitarization of northern areas associated with the National Pact enabled ex-combatants to link up with cocaine traffickers operating out of Guinea-Bissau" (Hannah Armstrong, "Crisis in Mali: Root Causes and Long-Term Solutions," Washington, D.C.: U.S. Institute of Peace, Brief 149, May 31, 2013, p. 2).

Conclusion

The above overview should underscore a few important characteristics of the conflict in northern Mali. Above all, it should make clear that the unrest has been largely limited to members of a few clans in one clan confederation (the Kel Adagh) that is part of one northern ethnic community (the Tuareg). Other Tuareg and non-Tuareg have mostly been bystanders, with the notable exception of the 1991–1996 conflict. This is important because it underlines that armed groups and, eventually, peace signatories far from represent northern Mali as a whole. It also highlights the fact that tensions with Bamako are only one cause of the conflict. Competition among northern Malians to advance their individual and group interests also plays a key role in fueling the various rebellions that have taken place over the years. Taking up arms is a means of economic, political, and social advancement. In northern Mali as elsewhere, "all politics is local."

CHAPTER THREE

Explaining the Failure of Past Peace Accords

For many northern Malians, the explanation for the failure of previous peace accords is simple: Bamako never followed through. A Malian Arab notable interviewed for this study described the problem in the following terms:

> Peace didn't hold in the past because it's like in a marriage. There will be problems, but, so long as they work at it, they'll be fine. The problem is that, with Mali, one of the partners had no interest in making things work.[1]

Although there is much to be said for this argument, the reality has been far more complicated and merits more consideration. This chapter examines the main challenges that have crippled peace-accord implementation: the lack of representation of the armed group that negotiated each of the peace accords; the nature of the grievances at the root of the rebellions; the shortcomings of democratization and decentralization; Bamako's limited legitimacy in Mali's most-remote regions; persistent insecurity; and, finally, the lack of transitional justice.

---

[1]   Arab leader B, interview with Michael Shurkin, Bamako, October 8, 2013.

Lack of Representativeness: Who Is Signing the Peace Accords?

As discussed above, the armed groups involved in Mali's insurrections in each instance have never represented more than a small minority of the north's inhabitants. Each generally represented specific slices or *fractions* of the northern communities, to use the old French colonial administrative term; each accord was struck with a different group, which thus represented some members of a different fraction. Not only are armed groups not representative of the northern populations, but those individuals who entered negotiations with the Malian government on behalf of the armed groups might not have been representative of most of their communities.[2] For example, the Tamanrasset, Algiers, and Ouagadougou Accords were all between the Malian state and one or two rebel groups that represented at most a few fractions. The 1992 National Pact stands out as an exception in that it involved a broader coalition of armed groups, yet we know that the negotiations took place against a backdrop of intense jostling among them for relative advantage, and collectively—in the absence of any democratic process—a coalition of groups that represents some members of some fractions cannot be said to represent all or even most northerners.

What Is Driving the Fighting?

The role of different and specific fractions in northern Mali's unrest and resulting peace accords points to three fundamental problems. The first is that only some portions of northern Malian society have regarded themselves as having been a party to the different negotiations and having benefited from the peace accords. The second is that the conflicts have been, at most, only partially driven by grievances against the Malian state. They have been driven at least as much by internal politics and reflect the ambitions of some groups or individuals

---

[2] Hélène Claudot-Hawad, "La fragmentation touarègue ou le prix de la 'paix,'" in Hélène Claudot-Hawad, ed., *Touaregs: Voix solitaires sous l'horizon confisqué*, Paris: Ethnies/Survival International, 1996, pp. 37–53, p. 42.

within them to promote themselves and their interests vis-à-vis others. This was most obviously the case with the 2006 rebellion, which can be described as the bid by an upstart Kel Adagh clan (the Ifergoumessen) to raise its status, as well as an act of entrepreneurship on the part of the rebellion's leaders. As a result, even if the Malian state fulfilled its part of negotiated peace accords, interfraction conflict could remain, as would the emergence of taking up arms as a viable means to advance one's personal or group interests in a land with few legitimate means to do so. The third issue is a general fragmentation of northern Malian society such that existing sources of authority, be they traditional chiefs or upstart rebel commanders, lack the means to impose their will on subordinate groups. As a result, such authorities cannot prevent other parts of northern Malian society from attempting to strike their own deals with the state.

It does not help that Mali's leadership since 1991, like the French colonial state, has consistently preferred to deal with the north by coopting certain northern elites, primarily by granting certain privileges in exchange for their cooperation. According to Jennifer Seely, co-option was one of the conscious objectives of the 1990s democratization and decentralization plan.[3] Initially, in the 1990s, Bamako's choice was to favor the Kel Adagh elites, the same elites who had won France's favor during the colonial period, most notably the amenokal's family and Ghaly. As president, ATT abruptly switched clients in 2008, dropping the aristocratic Ghaly for then–Lieutenant Colonel Gamou, an integrated former leader of a militia that represented the Imghad (commoners) in their conflict in the 1990s against the elites championed by Ghaly. Gamou essentially reactivated his militia and crushed the rebels, who were dominated by the aristocratic Ifergoumessen clan.

A Bellah community leader interviewed for this study put the problem succinctly:

> There is, in the population, a desire for change that is exploited by individuals. When these individuals take that [desire], they

---

[3] Jennifer C. Seely, "A Political Analysis of Decentralisation: Coopting the Tuareg Threat in Mali," *Journal of Modern African Studies*, Vol. 39, No. 3, 2001, pp. 499–524, p. 500.

go into rebellion, but, instead of fighting for the aspirations of people, it is for the interests of some individuals. When they have accords, it is for the material interest of a rebel chief or those who are in rebellion. But the problem remains. What is the problem? In the north, it is that the state identifies a few individuals and creates ties with them. These individuals . . . There's generally one with whom the state deals. That's a problem. The rest of the population isn't concerned, while the government only worries about taking care of the one person. So, frustrations and needs grow. There is a feeling of rejection.

Interestingly, several of the notables interviewed for this study compared the approach of the French colonial regime favorably to Mali's. Both, they said, picked a few individuals to be their intermediaries and empowered them to some extent. But whereas the French selected traditional fraction chiefs and gave them even more authority than they had traditionally, the independent Malian state, for a variety of reasons, usually selected individuals who not only lacked the intrinsic legitimacy of the traditional chiefs but also threatened their authority and often were hostile to the society's established hierarchies.[4] Bamako's anointed interlocutors were therefore doubly ineffective: They were not empowered by the communities they purported to represent, and they threatened the positions and interests of leaders who were so empowered. The French, according to an Arab leader, studied the population carefully and how northern society worked and only then made their choices.[5] A Tuareg notable similarly argued that, whereas the French were generally careful about the choices they made, Mali "makes bad choices," uninformed choices, or, worse, choices intended to disrupt northern society. Thus, according to Salair Touré, the mayor of Bara in Songa Circle, ATT created new powers that went against the traditional chiefs (*chefferie*), "but that is no way to organize a society . . . you need hierarchy."[6]

---

[4]   Bellah leader, 2013; Songhai leader A, phone interview with Michael Shurkin, October 8, 2013.

[5]   Arab leader A, 2013.

[6]   Songhai leader A, 2013.

Community leaders interviewed for this study also noted an important difference between pre-1960 Mali and post-1960 Mali that made the clientelist approach not only less effective but also more damaging with respect to the traditional social hierarchies. Specifically, northern society had changed such that people became much less amenable to being controlled by a few individuals of any sort. Now, explained a Bellah leader, individuals want emancipation from groups, and traditionally subordinate groups want to escape their condition: "There is a thirst for more equity," so no matter whom one chooses, "there are problems."[7] Last, an Arab leader noted that, although the French were outsiders, they were clearly perceived as the "dominant force," and, "at the time, there was a clear interest in working with the dominant force." Bamako, it seems, might not enjoy the same status.

When comparing contemporary Mali and colonial Mali, it must also be remembered that, at the time of the French conquest of northern Mali (1894–1916), the region was relatively neatly divided up by clan, caste, and ethnic group, making it easy for the French to identify leaders who clearly spoke for their communities—traditional *chefs de fraction*, such as amenokals, emirs, and other leaders who had established their legitimacy over the decades and centuries through various combinations of clerical and martial supremacy. There were also relatively well-established and legible hierarchies. The French learned to "read" the taxonomies of northern Malian society and manipulated it for their purposes.[8] They also reified the hierarchies of the day and preserved the status quo up until the day they left.

Decolonization removed these obstacles to societal evolution. Since then, a combination of Malian government policy, droughts, and a variety of social and demographic trends (such as migration abroad and urbanization) have had the effect of undermining traditional authorities and eroding the structures and divisions that had, for so long, characterized northern Malian life. Indeed, much of the strife

---

[7] Bellah leader, 2013.

[8] On how Libya used a similar method to emphasize divisions within the exiled Tuareg community to keep their independentist and military ambitions in check, see Claudot-Hawad, 1996, p. 41.

that has afflicted northern Mali since 1991 can be explained by the will of certain groups and leaders to contest traditional hierarchies and that of others to defend them. More recently, "reformist" Islam (i.e., movements to combat traditional Malian Sufi religion with so-called purer forms of Islam), which arrived in northern Mali in the late 1990s, has added to the challenge against established leaders—many of whom anchor their legitimacy in religious credentials. The phenomenon of armed struggle most likely has also added to the general overturning of tradition in that it has provided young men with new avenues of social and economic advancement, as has the influx of international aid organizations, whose money has, in some ways, become just another resource to contest.

The rise of narcotics trafficking has also generated new solidarities while corroding older ones. According to a Sahel expert, even compared with the area in the 1990s, northern Malian society has fragmented, largely because of criminality and trafficking:

> Things are not as simple as [they were in] the 1990s. There were very strong individual trajectories. Around those individuals, certain groups coalesced. But the big change is the importance of money. He who has money can bring people together, independently of fraction, etc.[9]

Mali scholar Judith Scheele similarly has noted that trafficking has brought wealth to some historically subordinate groups, which has encouraged them to challenge their traditional superiors. The example she cites is of the Tilemsi Arabs, the traditional vassals of the Kunta Arabs in the Gao region. According to Scheele, in 2002, the non-Kunta Arabs, because of the wealth recently acquired by their involvement in cigarette and weapon trafficking, felt sufficiently confident to challenge Kunta domination over them, leading to electoral confrontations and violence.[10] More starkly, Scheele adds, "fraud has led to questioning, sometimes violently, the political hierarchies of the region; it permits

---

[9]   Sahel expert A, phone interview with Michael Shurkin, December 11, 2012.

[10] Judith Scheele, "Tribus, états et fraude: La région frontalière algéro-malienne," *Études rurales*, Vol. 184, February 2009, pp. 79–94, p. 86.

the young, ready to risk their life, to become independent and to over-turn familial hierarchies."[11]

The traditional forms of social organization, such as clans and caste, nonetheless have not disappeared; experts agree that traditional authorities and fraction/tribal/clan lines and hierarchies still matter. According to Scheele, for examples, understanding tribes, "far from being the only frame of reference, remains fundamental for under-standing conflicts and solidarities, and above all, for explaining and judging them."[12] However, they have lost whatever monopoly they might have had as authorities or sources of identity, meaning that they compete with a diverse array of other authorities, creating options and, occasionally, frictions.

Flawed Decentralization and Democracy

Many Malian politicians, civil-society leaders, and northern groups have reflexively argued that what Mali needs is more decentralization and more democracy, based on the assumption that insufficient quan-tities of both have contributed to Mali's instability. The International Crisis Group, for example, noted that "decentralization today consti-tutes the favored reply by the government and its partners not only for responding to the feeling of marginalization in the north but also to engage in a greater reform of governance."[13] In October 2013, the Malian government sponsored a national forum on decentralization (États généraux de la décentralisation), a large event that brought repre-sentatives from many diverse Malian communities to discuss the state of Malian governance. The consensus that emerged was, in brief, that

---

[11] Scheele, 2009, p. 91.

[12] Scheele, 2009, p. 88. Charles Grémont and Pierre Boilley have also insisted on the impor-tance of the traditional divisions.

[13] International Crisis Group, *Mali: Reform or Relapse*, Brussels, Africa Report 210, Janu-ary 10, 2014, p. 29.

Mali needed more democracy and more decentralization.[14] Basically, the logic is that the more communes, the more elected positions; and the more elected positions, the greater the representativeness, responsiveness, and legitimacy of the government.

This logic is at odds with Mali's experience with decentralization and democratization following the 1992 National Pact, which suggests that the call for "more" democracy should be replaced by the call for "better" democracy. It appears that, at least in the near term, decentralization and democratization often accentuate "the intensity of the struggle for access to local power."[15] The International Crisis Group points out that local communities have yet to internalize the political culture that comes with liberal democracy, including electoral competition and the idea that politics need not be a zero-sum game. Thus, "decentralization sometimes generates a radicalization of community demands and violent tensions around the territory's administrative divisions."[16] Similarly, Mali expert David Gutelius has observed,

> decentralisation also intensified the internal struggles for power within northern communities, with winner-take-all outcomes in resource and aid access. . . . [F]urther, the blanket form in which decentralisation was implemented without taking into account how local northern institutions already operated continues to make success elusive.[17]

---

[14] Be Coulibaly, "États généraux de la décentralisation: Des recommandations pour mieux faire," *L'essor*, November 1, 2013; "Mali: Bilan positif pour les États généraux de la décentralisation," *Radio France internationale*, October 24, 2013; Assane Koné, "Résolution de la crise malienne: Recommandations des états généraux de la décentralisation," *Notre nation*, October 28, 2013.

[15] International Crisis Group, 2014, p. 29.

[16] International Crisis Group, 2014, p. 29.

[17] David Gutelius, "Islam in Northern Mali and the War on Terror," *Journal of Contemporary African Studies*, Vol. 25, No. 1, 2007, pp. 59–76, p. 4.

A Berabiche Arab leader described in more-concrete terms the ways in which decentralization pitted northern communities against each other:

> Decentralization was profaned because there was no competence transferred. Rather, it emphasized the local divisions. That's what happened at Kidal [and elsewhere with the] Kunta and Arab [communities]. Kuntas wanted to strengthen their hegemony, whereas Arabs wanted their own voice.[18]

Electoral competition and clan rivalry become intertwined, as illustrated by an incident in June 1999 when former MPA leader Bahanga of the Ifergoumessen clan abducted an electoral committee during communal elections because of a long-standing land dispute with rival clans around the Tejerert wells.[19] Elections in Mali and elsewhere have been shown to increase competition among factions desirous to capture elected positions for their own purposes, and some groups and leaders, among them the amenokal's family and other elites, have successfully captured elected offices in a bid to shore up and legitimate their traditional power.

One of the most-provocative analyses of what transpired in the 1990s is by German Mali expert Georg Klute and the late sociologist Trutz von Trotha, who argued that democratization and decentralization in Mali and elsewhere in post-1991 Africa enabled leading chiefdoms—such as the elite Kel Adagh clans in Mali—to assert "parasovereignty" at the expense of the much-compromised sovereignty of the central state.[20] The "parastate" chiefdom, they assert, uses all the opportunities that democracy and decentralization afford it to put into positions of power people who are loyal to it—in Mali's case, the elite

---

[18] Berabiche leader, 2013. *Kunta* and *Arab* are sometimes used interchangeably. However, in this specific context, *Arab* refers to non-Kunta Arabs who historically have been politically subordinate to the Kuntas.

[19] Florquin and Pezard, 2005, p. 62, based on written correspondence with Lecocq, January 2005.

[20] Trutz von Trotha and Georg Klute, "Von der Postkolonie zur Parastaatlichkeit: Das Beispiel Schwarzafrika," *Jahrbuch für internationale Sicherheitspolitik*, 2001, p. 8.

Kel Ifoghas (i.e., the clans at the head of the Kel Adagh), often by rigging elections. One result of this approach is the "territorialization" of the chiefdom's dominance once power and revenue become associated with specific electoral and administrative boundaries.[21]

A leader of the Arab Berabiche community in Mali put the problem more sympathetically and less dramatically in an interview for this study. Traditional chiefs, he said, felt threatened by democracy and thus worked hard to capture it by getting involved in electoral politics, which had the effect of blocking political progress.[22] They often have good reason to feel threatened because numerous historically subordinate communities have used elections to challenge the dominance of other groups. For example, in the confrontation between Tilemsi Arabs and their Kunta overlords observed by Scheele, the Tilemsi Arabs won the election in 2004, prompting them to stop paying their feudal *jizya* tax to the Kuntas, according to Scheele.[23] Some Kuntas then fled to Kidal, where they are among their traditional allies, the Kel Adagh. Although the available evidence suggests that no group in northern Mali, including the Kel Adagh amenokal's family, has fully achieved the kind of parasovereignty of which Trotha and Klute warned, this is not for lack of trying, and other factions within northern Malian society resent the elites' aspirations and have resisted.

Additionally, decentralization has been plagued by a set of more-prosaic problems, among them a lack of financial resources and human capital, which impede newly created administrations and their elected members from accomplishing much of anything. Susanna Wing and Bréhima Kassibo have documented the numerous fiscal and administrative obstacles preventing the effective functioning of the system as intended.[24] In Wing's words, "Unfortunately, in decentralization, the weak Malian national government produced weak local governments

---

[21] Trotha and Klute, 2001, p. 9.

[22] Berabiche leader, 2013.

[23] Scheele, 2009, p. 86.

[24] Wing and Kassibo, 2014.

with limited capacity."[25] Moreover, she writes, "the project was flawed by the lack of resources and the questionable commitment of elites to real decentralization that would increase the government's accountability to the people."[26] According to a Kel Antsar Tuareg leader and former high-level Malian government official who corroborated Wing's assessment, decentralization meant going from 19 to 703 communes, while the resources allotted to them did not increase commensurately.[27] Worse, he said, inflation has lessened the value of what the communes did receive. As a result, he argued for reducing the number of communes, unlike many other northern leaders who, for political reasons, instead support an *increase* in the number of communes.

Limited Legitimacy of Bamako

Some observers have noted the Malian state's lack of popular legitimacy among northern populations, a lacking that arguably fuels resentment against Bamako and encourages northerners to continue to think in terms of "us versus them."

Most have associated the government's poor standing with a failure to provide services, which reflects a commonly held belief that service provision is an important, if not primary, means by which states legitimize themselves. The International Crisis Group makes the argument for service provision particularly clear:

The state . . . lost its credibility in the eyes of a large portion of the populations of these regions, even if the majority does not support the separatist or autonomist project of the armed groups. To reconcile the state and its citizens, the rehabilitations programs

---

[25] Wing, 2013, p. 7.

[26] Wing, 2013, p. 7.

[27] Tuareg leader and former high-level Malian government official, interview with Michael Shurkin, October 5, 2013.

that are starting must focus on concrete services provided to the population. The state must not miss its return to the North.[28]

The International Crisis Group cites evidence of general discontentment with governance, such as protests in Gao in October and November 2013 against government corruption, ineffectiveness, and insecurity.[29] In fact, Gao has seen the emergence of a variety of political movements—Jeunes Patriotes, Jeune Patrouille, and Nous Pas Bouger—which are associated with youth and the Songhai community and are dedicated to promoting the interests of their community while criticizing the Malian state for its failings.[30]

Such a view is consistent with the argument that failed implementation doomed past peace accords. Again, there is some truth to that. However, legitimacy has to do with much more than service provision and governance. Nations are invented and represent a "daily plebiscite" among people who agree to share in "the idea that there exists a political domain that is independent of the interests of individuals and that they must respect the rules according to which it runs."[31] There has to be an idea of the nation that is confirmed by political institutions and processes. Elections are important for that, although they take time to shape political culture and national identity.[32] Schools are also critical to the fostering of the idea of the nation and the inculcation of it among the young.[33] Armies, too, have historically have been particularly important as crucibles for the formation of national identities, and

---

[28] International Crisis Group, 2014, p. i.

[29] International Crisis Group, 2014, p. 14.

[30] Mohamed Lamine, "Gao: La population en meeting de protestation contre le gouvernement de transition," *Ouest Afrika Blog*, June 5, 2013; HCME Allemagne, "Jeunes patriotes de Gao," *YouTube*, November 25, 2012; Madiassa Kaba Diakité, "Les jeunes de Gao se désolent du manque de reconnaissance de l'état," *Le républicain*, April 15, 2013; "Manifestation à Gao: Quand les revendications se font sociales," *Radio France internationale*, October 11, 2013.

[31] Dominique Schnapper, *La communauté des citoyens: Sur l'idée moderne de nation*, Paris: Gallimard, 1994, p. 44.

[32] Schnapper, 1994, p. 97.

[33] Schnapper, 1994, p. 131.

indeed Malians acknowledge that the integration of northerners into the Malian army since 1991 was an important start. As a Berabiche notable put it,

> The integration of combatants was a good thing. It allowed some representation of the north in the army. Mali was never a nation. We never built a nation, in which those from Kaye and from Kidal share the same values. Young northerners aren't interested in politics; politics never interested them.[34]

However the idea of the nation is cultivated, it must be inclusive such that all can see themselves in it. Yet some of the notables interviewed for this study expressed frustration, both because they feel that the current idea of the Malian nation fostered by southern Malians and the Malian state offers them no place and because they perceive the Malian state as slighting them in various ways and treating them as, at best, second-class citizens. According to Lecocq, the problem has its roots at least as far back as Mali's independence, when the country's new leaders elaborated a national identity that excluded the north:

> As a basis to imagine a Malian nation, the regime used the rich history of the area [they] controlled, naming the country after one of Africa's most important medieval empires and presenting itself, if not as a direct continuation of this empire, then at least as its rightful heir. Other elements used were cultural, taken from the heartland of the new state, the Mande and Bambara areas. . . . The consequence was that the nation was not just imagined as Malian, but even more specifically as Mande. But the Malian leaders' wish for state control and their image of the nation along Mande lines proved incompatible with these same leaders' ideas about and images of potential members of that nation—the Kel Tamasheq.[35]

---

[34] Berabiche leader, 2013.

[35] Lecocq, 2002, p. 96.

Lecocq further characterizes Malian national identity as being construed in opposition to stereotypes about northern Malians: "Policies in the North were primarily based on positive stereotyped images of the Mande as the Malian nation, and the negative stereotyped images of the Kel Tamasheq as a 'savage other' in need of social and economic development."[36]

It should not be surprising, then, that, according to the head of a Tuareg culture organization from Kidal, Tuareg "get annoyed" when members of Mali's dominant ethnic group, the Bambara, who largely control the government, evoke the memory of past Bambara empires as fundamental to Malian national identity: "We need a new definition of the nation that includes us."[37] An Arab leader described the problem in terms of how the Malian state related to northerners, especially the Arab community. Invariably, he argued, despite Arabs' sincere desire to be a part of the Malian nation, Mali would reinforce their feeling that they were "second degree citizens."[38] Similarly, an Arab notable complained that the Malian army "goes around with interpreters who do not know the local language. . . . People don't understand that."[39] Lastly, another Arab notable observed that the state has been partisan to intercommunal conflicts, picking sides rather than trying to build the nation and "attract everyone."[40]

Another Arab interviewed, a deserted colonel who joined the FIAA and subsequently the Arab Movement of Azawad (Mouvement arabe de l'Azawad [MAA]) in the 1990s, described having had a full career in the Malian army but feeling compelled to defect to an Arab militia after the army "abandoned" the Arab community in 2012, leaving it to the MNLA and the Islamists.[41] Another interviewee likewise

---

[36] Lecocq, 2002, p. 96.

[37] Tuareg cultural association president, interview with Michael Shurkin, Bamako, October 8, 2013.

[38] Berabiche leader, 2013.

[39] Berabiche leader, 2013.

[40] Arab leader A, 2013.

[41] MAA commander, interview with Michael Shurkin, Bamako, October 8, 2013.

pointed to a trend toward falling back on one's solidarity groups in response to the stresses created by instability and insecurity.[42] This happened in the 1990s as initially united rebel movements fragmented into what ultimately were clan and tribal militias (the MPA and Gamou's ARLA being notable examples). The tendency only gained strength as a result of the events of 2012 when, according to the Arabs interviewed for this study, the Malian state ceased to exist in the north, leaving the Arab communities on their own to contend with the MNLA and the Islamists.

Interviewees' comments suggest that the perceived abandonment of the north by the Malian state was a significant blow because it signified not just a military defeat but, more critically, a failure to regard the north and its inhabitants as an integral part of Mali. It also created the immediate problem of defending northern communities' interests. "The army fled the north, and it was dangerous," noted an Arab leader.[43] The MAA colonel present during the leader's interview similarly claimed that he deserted only after the army fled and abandoned the Arab community.[44] The leader associated Mali's abandonment of the north not just with the MAA's genesis but also a portion of the public support the Islamist group Movement for Unity and Jihad in West Africa (MUJWA) has been able to enjoy in the Gao region. People, he said, reckoned that Mali was finished and completely rejected the MNLA and the Tuareg-led Islamist group Ansar Dine, leaving them with little choice but to side with MUJWA.[45] One reason for Arabs' pessimism regarding Mali, he added, was that ATT had already made it absolutely clear in recent years that he was not going to "lift a finger to help," meaning that there was little point in resisting the Islamists.[46] People would not dare do it alone. The leader claimed that northern-

---

[42] Berabiche leader, 2013.

[43] Arab leader B, 2013.

[44] MAA commander, 2013.

[45] Arab leader B, 2013.

[46] The International Crisis Group also noted the prevalent feeling of abandonment. See International Crisis Group, 2014, p. 14.

ers would defend themselves against Islamists if they thought that the state or someone else was serious about helping them.

An important result of the 2012–2013 events is a heightening of conflict among northern Mali's different communities. Those interviewed insist that, until recently, everyone more or less got along and that the divisions among the groups are new. Although this is likely an exaggeration, the crisis has revealed the acuteness of antagonisms pitting various subgroups (e.g., Idnan, Berabiche, Tilemsi Arab) against one another.[47] According to the International Crisis Group, "the gulf between communities" has expanded in part because of the accumulation of resentment, the sentiment of impunity, and the progressive erosion of local reconciliation mechanisms.[48] Notwithstanding the integration of northerners and the prominence within the army of some northern commanders, most interviewees point to conflict and the negative role of the Malian army, which both aggravate the sense of insecurity and reinforce northerners' resentment toward Bambara-dominated southern Mali.

More broadly speaking, several described the evolution in terms of *communautarisme*, meaning that members of different communities saw themselves more as members of a particular solidarity group—e.g., tribe, clan, ethnicity—and less as members of a larger and more abstract community of citizens. The Berabiche leader interviewed for this study described communautarisme as being "an inward retreat in the face of injustice," with the result that people close themselves off to members of other communities.[49] A state that inspires such a reaction among its minority communities is undermining national unity, not building it.

---

[47] International Crisis Group, 2014, p. 12.

[48] International Crisis Group, 2014, p. 12.

[49] Berabiche leader, 2013.

Persistent Insecurity

As of 2014, the problem of insecurity still stands out as a primary concern for the residents of northern Mali. Nearly all of the community leaders and experts interviewed for this study in Bamako cited insecurity as a key issue. Indeed, one of the critical problems in the north is that, absent security and a force capable of providing it, northerners will do what they feel they must or is otherwise in their best interest, which might mean turning to an armed group, a self-defense militia, an organized criminal gang, or one of the remaining Islamist groups for protection. Thus, insecurity is both cause and effect, creating a vicious cycle.

Northerners perceive three sources of insecurity, or three sides of the security problem: criminal and jihadist groups, from drug traffickers to al Qaeda in the Islamic Maghreb (AQIM) and MUJWA; rival communities; and, to a lesser extent, the Malian army.

Some northerners acknowledge that the demilitarization of the region as per the 1992 National Pact helped foster insecurity. As a Tuareg leader and former high-level Malian government official put it, "One completely killed the army's ability to conduct its mission of defending the territory."[50] As of 2014, Mali's partners, chief among them France and the European Union, were busy training the Malian army. However, northern Malians also see the Malian army as not only incapable of protecting them but perhaps at least as much of a threat as, say, AQIM, whose members have built up strong community ties over the past 15 years. There have been allegations of collusion between the Malian military and the Ganda Koy and Ganda Izo self-defense militias, which engaged in attacks on Arab and Tuareg civilians in the 1990s.[51] Lecocq describes Ganda Koy has having been founded and led by ostensibly deserted Malian army officers who continued to wear their uniforms and who enjoyed at least tacit support from the military.[52]

---

[50] Tuareg leader and former high-level Malian government official, 2013.

[51] See Lecocq, 2002, p. 272.

[52] See Lecocq, 2002, p. 272.

What becomes apparent is that the Malian army has two basic problems. One is its fecklessness and lack of cohesion—its inability to protect the country, provide security, and generate confidence in the state. The March 2012 mutiny and coup, the April "countercoup" attempt, subsequent intra-army fighting, a nearly unbroken series of defeats at the hands of rebels and Islamists, and serial mass defections have left no illusions about the Malian army's capabilities.[53] The other is that its presence is often a negative one in that it not only cannot defeat militants but also antagonizes the very people who might benefit from its protection. In the simplest terms, the Malian army must become cohesive and learn to fight but also to better serve Malian society and to become a unifying force rather than a divisive one. Operational readiness, the usual metric applied to armies with respect to their training and capabilities, is necessary but not sufficient. The Malian army needs to be *républicaine*—in the French sense of the term—and not just effective (particularly while French and United Nations [UN] troops in the country can handle the more-critical security threats). A republican army is, as the International Crisis Group observed, one that obeys its chain of command and respects its civilian overseers.[54] But it is also more than that. It is a force that at least symbolically embodies the values of the republic and fosters them, which, in Mali's case, must include the embrace of its diverse population. As an Arab leader put it,

> The question of the army is very important for us. The army has to be interethnic, diverse. It must be republican. . . . For us, for the army to be strong, it has to be, fundamentally, a certain kind of army. Multiethnic and above divisions.[55]

Historically speaking, forming a republican army is something most Western militaries do as a matter of course. It involves instill-

[53] For more on the Malian army's internal problems, see Andrew McGregor, "Red Berets, Green Berets: Can Mali's Divided Military Restore Order and Stability?" *Terrorism Monitor*, Vol. 11, No. 4, February 22, 2013.

[54] International Crisis Group, 2014, p. 32.

[55] Arab leader A, 2013.

ing a certain kind of patriotism and cultivating particular ideas and values related to national identity. It also involves promoting on merit rather than connections. A republican army draws on all elements of the population, instills a sense of civic identity and national service, and requires submission to elected civilian authorities.

Absence of Justice and Reconciliation

A final issue is the lack of justice with respect to basic criminality; abuses by the Malian state against civilians; and abuses by various Malian groups and communities against one another, as well as against civilians. The 1992 National Pact addressed this issue by calling for the creation of an investigative commission charged with looking into "the crimes perpetrated against the civilian populations," although there is no evidence that this commission was actually created. The other accords do not address justice-related issues at all.

When northern Malians talk of impunity, they mean it in two senses: impunity with regard to criminality, such as corruption and trafficking, and impunity with regard to abuses, both by the Malian army against civilians and by different communities against one another. The former problem has been well documented. Mali ranked 127 out of 177 countries in Transparency International's 2013 Corruption Perceptions Index.[56] The World Bank's Worldwide Governance Indicators give a similarly bleak view of Mali's corruption levels and place the country in only the 30th percentile for rule of law.[57] Similarly, it is widely believed that the Malian state has, at the very least, shown itself to be remarkably tolerant of trafficking. "No one has been punished for drugs," complained an Arab leader.[58] Many sources go further and accuse the state of colluding with traffickers and other illicit actors,

---

[56] Transparency International, "Corruption by Country/Territory: Mali," undated (a); referenced July 14, 2014.

[57] World Bank, "Country Data Report for Mali, 1996–2012," c. 2013; referenced July 14, 2014.

[58] Berabiche leader, 2013.

including some of the Arab communities in the Timbuktu region and Tilemsi. For example, a Berabiche notable claimed that the Malian state created the MAA to defend certain business interests, and he added that Bamako has consistently acted in ways that exacerbated intercommunal tensions in pursuit of pecuniary interests.[59] Whether true or not, these types of allegations reflect perceptions of bad faith on the part of the Malian state and ATT's administration, as well as cynicism regarding the state's interest in promoting stability and development.

The latter problem is more challenging because it speaks to the fact that, at this point, there are at least 20 years of rancor built up among different northern Malian communities, resulting from crimes both real and imagined. All agree on the need for reconciliation and ways to move forward more peacefully, although it is not obvious how. For one thing, the Malian state is itself regarded as too partisan and thus incapable of arbitrating. For another, reconciliation would require recognizing past acts of violence, which could reopen wounds.[60] Justice might also conflict with other legitimate political needs, such as encouraging certain armed factions to negotiate when some might prefer to arrest them. Justice and reconciliation are particularly important topics in the wake of the Ouagadougou Accord because of the numerous abuses that were committed in 2012 and 2013. Human Rights Watch provides a long list of such abuses by armed groups:

> summary executions of up to 153 Malian soldiers in Aguelhok by armed groups that occupied the north; widespread looting and pillage, and sexual violence by the MNLA; and the recruitment and use of child combatants, amputations, and destruction of shrines by Islamist armed groups.[61]

It adds: "Malian soldiers were also implicated in numerous abuses during the 2013 offensive to take back the north, including 26 extrajudicial executions, 11 enforced disappearances, and over 70 cases of

---

[59] Berabiche leader, 2013.

[60] International Crisis Group, 2014, p. 35.

[61] Human Rights Watch, "Mali: Ensure Justice for Grave Abuses," March 21, 2014.

torture or ill-treatment of suspected Islamist rebels."[62] None has yet been addressed by the new Malian government.

---

[62] Human Rights Watch, 2014.

CHAPTER FOUR

Moving Forward

The preceding discussion of Mali's problems and the failings of previous peace accords has highlighted several specific areas of concern. These include, above all, insecurity, the need for greater representativeness, and effective ways to bring local communities into the management of their own affairs. These three elements are all related because most sources consider representation and participation the key not only to crafting peace agreements in which a preponderance of northern Malians see their interests addressed but also to maintaining security. Northern Malian interviewees agree, for example, that northerners themselves, not the Malian state, the United Nations, or the French, are most capable of securing the region. These issues are also tied to appropriate reform of the army—with its "republicanization" being perceived as more important than its tactical competence—and the end of impunity.

Building Representativeness: Democracy

One thing that must be emphasized is that, notwithstanding the widespread criticism of decentralization and democratization, all sources agree that both are essential, even if some of the modalities need to be altered. Democracy remains Mali's best hope in the long term. Indeed, all those interviewed for this study, as well as other sources, have agreed that elected officials must not be counted out and have to be assumed to enjoy at least some legitimacy and representativeness. A prominent Tuareg who played a key role in the PSPSDN program reacted with indignation during an interview at the suggestion that northerners do not have a voice in government. "It's false to say that communities do not have a voice," he said.[1] "They absolutely have a voice—all the elected officials and representatives."

An examination of Mali's most recent election, the legislative election held in November 2013, bears out the claim that elected officials are not to be discounted in any search for legitimate northern voices. According to the election data published on *aBamako.com*, roughly 56 percent of northern Mali's registered voters participated in the legislative election.[2] Northern Mali has 630,000 registered voters and an estimated total population of 1.3 million (according to the 2009 census). Some 350,000 voted, or 27 percent of the population. If we look more closely at the votes in specific regions and circles, we find a variety of outcomes. First, incumbents represented fewer than half of the victors, suggesting that no particular clique or caste has a lock on National Assembly seats.[3] Second, if we can judge by the victors' names and party affiliations, they are fairly diverse with respect to the communities they represent.

The results from the four circles of the Kidal region, where Kel Adagh Tuareg have historically been politically dominant, although not necessarily a numerical majority, are particularly interesting in showing a diversity of electoral results:[4] Of the four victors of the 2013 legislative elections, three are Tuareg, the fourth is Songhai. However, the Tuareg victors come from different factions within the Tuareg community:

- Kidal's circle winner, Ahmoudene Ag Iknass, hails from the Imghad or commoner caste, which has often been in opposition

---

[1] Tuareg notable, phone interview with Michael Shurkin, October 4, 2013.

[2] For election data, see "Liste des nouveaux députés: Mali," *aBamako.com*, undated.

[3] As a comparison, note that 90 percent of incumbents seeking reelection to the U.S. House of Representatives in 2012 won (Greg Giroux, "Voters Throw Bums in While Holding Congress in Disdain," *Bloomberg*, December 13, 2012).

[4] Malian administrative divisions are, in ascending order of size, the commune, the circle, and the region.

to the Kel Ifogha nobility and is associated with Gamou. One press report describes Iknass as the "coordinator" of the Imghad.[5] It also notes that Iknass, as with the Imghad in general and certainly Gamou, is loyal to the Malian state and has three sons in the Malian military. Iknass won 65.3 percent of the vote, which put him ahead of his two competitors, Inawelène Ag Ahmed, who fought with the MNLA and won 32.2 percent of the vote, and Manayete Ag Mohamed, who won 2.5 percent.[6] Iknass's victory represents a victory for nonnobles and perhaps is indicative of the abstention of voters aligned with the noble clans who support the amenokal's family and are associated with the HCUA. Indeed, voter turnout in Kidal's circle, at 28 percent, was low compared with that in many other areas. The elites made a stronger showing in Kidal's Abeïbara and Tin-Essako circles.[7]

- In Abeïbara, the HCUA-affiliated Ahmada Ag Bibi won 96.7 percent of the vote, with the turnout was reported at 71 percent of registered voters. In Tin-Essako, Mohamed Ag Intallah, one of the amenokal's sons, won 100 percent of the mere 102 votes cast—a total of 14 percent of the registered voters in tiny Tin-Essako. No one ran against him.[8]

- Finally, Tessalit's victor was a Songhai woman, Aïcha Belco Maïga, who defeated a female Tuareg candidate with 64.5 percent of the vote, with a 62-percent reported turnout rate. Until recently the president of Tessalit's council, she is a critic of the MNLA.[9]

---

[5] D. Djire, "Situation à Kidal: Les vérités du député Ahmoudène AG Iknass," *L'essor*, December 27, 2013.

[6] "Liste des nouveaux députés: Kidal," *aBamako.com*, undated.

[7] "Liste des nouveaux députés: Abeibara," *aBamako.com*, undated; "Liste des nouveaux députés: Tin-Essako," *aBamako.com*, undated.

[8] "Liste des nouveaux députés: Tin-Essako," undated.

[9] Amadou Salif Guindo, "Mme Assory Aicha Belco Maiga, présidente du conseil de cercle de Tessalit à propos de la libération de Gao 'Ma joie ne sera totale que quand Tombouctou et Kidal seront reprises,'" *La Dépêche*, January 30, 2013; "Liste des nouveaux députés: Tessalit," *aBamako.com*, undated.

The elections in ethnically diverse Gao similarly resulted in a fairly diverse group of representatives, although the winners appear to share antipathy toward the MNLA. For example, in Gao itself, Tuareg Assarid Ag Imbarcaouane, who won 55.9 percent of the vote, with a healthy 55.3-percent turnout, is an outspoken critic of the MNLA and last year told Malian television that "the populations of the north will never accept the return of the MNLA in the towns."[10] Gao's other two winners, Abouzeïdi Ousmane Maïga and Arbonkana Maïga, are both Songhai. The former, described as a "village chief" by one source, has also denounced the MNLA and the independence movement.[11] Looking more broadly at the entire Gao region, we find again a diverse array of groups and opinions represented. One of Bourem's two newly elected deputies, for example, Mohamed Ould Mataly, is commonly referred to as an Arab businessman who collaborated with MUJWA. Mataly himself denies that he has ties to MUJWA, but he has spoken sympathetically of it at least in terms of its having protected the population from the MNLA and being more in tune with its interests.[12] The other newly elected deputy from Bourem is an altogether different leader, Aïchata Alassane Cissé, a woman with clear anti-MUJWA and anti-MNLA credentials.

These results suggest that democracy and the electoral process, though far from perfect, at least have given some expression to different portions of the community. Turnout rates and other factors, such as the candidates' track records in their respective communities, suggest that the people elected have some legitimacy. They do not represent everyone, but they are not entirely unrepresentative, either.

---

[10] "L'honorable Assarid Ag Imbarcaouane sur l'ORTM: 'Les populations du nord n'accepteront jamais le retour du MNLA dans les villes,'" *L'indépendant*, February 11, 2013. Imbarcaouane hails from an Imghad clan, which appears to correlate with antipathy toward Kel Ifogha nobles.

[11] Roberto, "El gobierno del Azawad," *A modo de esperanza*, June 20, 2012.

[12] Chahana Takiou, "Entretien avec Mohamed Ould Mataly, ancien député de Bourem: 'Je ne suis pas du MUJAO,'" *22 Septembre*, July 12, 2012.

Building Representativeness: Involving Traditional Chiefs

Susanna Wing and Bréhima Kassibo have noted that the new political structures stood up by decentralization have left out the chieftaincies as such (although, like anyone else, chiefs can run for office), which they characterize as the "locus of real decentralized power in Mali."[13] They noted that, during last fall's national forum on decentralization, participants supported increasing the role of traditional authorities within communes, and a recent survey revealed that 82 percent of Malians stated that they have a great deal of trust for traditional authorities, whereas only 50 percent said the same about police and only 43 percent said the same about courts.[14] Thus it should not be surprising that interviewees consistently emphasized the need to involve traditional leaders in political and security matters to a degree not seen since the colonial period. Traditional leaders, these sources argued, would bring significant legitimacy and representativeness to political processes, and they could play important roles in mounting community-based security measures. As an Arab leader put it,

> The Malian army cannot secure the north. MINUSMA [United Nations Multidimensional Integrated Stabilization Mission in Mali] cannot do it. [French military operation] Serval cannot do it. We need the tribal chiefs. We have to entrust them again and give them a role in public affairs. And transparency.[15]

A Songhai leader and town mayor interviewed for this report made a similar remark and argued that, after having diminished the traditional chiefs among the Songhai, now the state needs to lean on them: "They have influence."[16] The president of a Tuareg cultural asso-

---

[13] Wing and Kassibo, 2014, p. 196.

[14] Wing and Kassibo, 2014, p. 196.

[15] Berabiche leader, 2013.

[16] Songhai leader B, phone interview with Michael Shurkin, February 11, 2014.

ciation was more explicit when he called for reverting to the colonial system and working through traditional chiefs.[17]

This does not, however, mean reverting to the clientelist approach pioneered in Mali by the French[18] and haphazardly practiced by Bamako, which consisted of empowering certain notables and certain factions to assert control. An appropriate political and security arrangement today would have to be done in the context of democracy and a general concern for equity, as well as the basic fact that not all traditional chiefs would make positive contributions or enhance the legitimacy of Mali's government.

The idea is that many of northern Mali's problems stem from the tension between traditional leaders and new ones, who clash in various arenas, including elections, with the result that the leaders resist democracy and old and new elites find themselves in conflict. Instead of having more democracy and more decentralization, the argument is in favor of supplementing the existing democratic mechanisms with some form of parallel institutions or councils that enable the tribal chiefs to participate without being in opposition to the state administration or elected officials. "Before [more] democratization," the Berabiche leader argued, "one must create a place with roles and responsibilities for the *chefs de fraction* within the administration." This place could be "perhaps a fractions chiefs council."[19]

One of the benefits that might accrue from finding new ways of involving traditional chiefs is that it might free up the chiefs to evolve. From their point of view, the problem in Kidal in particular, but also with important groups, such as the Kunta, is that traditional authorities have been operating in opposition to cultural and political changes that have been taking place around them.[20]

---

[17] Tuareg cultural association president, 2013.

[18] In fact, it was France's arrangement with the father of the current amenokal early in the last century, whereby the amenokal ensured the security of Mali's territory against Moroccan raiders that solidified the Kel Adagh's preeminence.

[19] Berabiche leader, 2013.

[20] Tuareg leader and former high-level Malian government official, 2013; Arab leader B, 2013.

The idea therefore is not restoring the place of traditional chiefs in lieu of democracy but promoting both at the same time. Indeed, our sources, despite their criticism of Mali's experience with democracy thus far, insist that democracy must go forward. Moreover, democracy, especially if traditional chiefs can find a place outside elected office, has the function of broadening representativeness. More to the point, all agree that elected officials in Mali do, in fact, enjoy a measure of legitimacy—perhaps not enough for the system to stand on its own without support from, for example, traditional chiefs.

It is important to note that involving traditional chiefs brings its own problems. Many might have discredited themselves over the years or simply lost whatever authority they or their predecessors might have had. There are also issues involved with identifying who the traditional chiefs are or dealing with rival claimants. For example, contestation over who succeeds the Kel Adagh amenokal and what his role should be is regarded has having some role in the events of the past few years. Finally, it must be noted that the commentaries of our interviewees might have been self-serving given that many of them can be described as traditional chiefs.

Building Representativeness: Dealing with Armed Groups

Yet to be addressed here are the armed groups and the halting negotiations between them and the Malian state. One of the fundamental mistakes of previous peace negotiations and the resulting agreements has been the apparent assumption that the rebel groups involved in negotiations speak for everyone in the north, when they actually speak for particular fractions or coalitions of fractions that represent, at best, no more than minorities within minorities. To cite a Tuareg notable, "Ouagadougou represents a negotiation between the state and the rebellion," while "the citizens have nothing to do with it."[21] Moreover, it is clear that many resent rebel groups or the fractions associated with them. Anti-MNLA sentiment, for example, is strong in many regions,

---

[21] Tuareg notable, 2013.

including Gao and Timbuktu, to the point that certain communities preferred to side with MUJWA because of its opposition to the MNLA. Fractional and ethnic lines shed some light on these divisions: The dividing line between the MNLA and MUJWA, as well as between them and the HCUA, following clear ethnic antagonisms, such as the conflict between Tilemsi Arabs (MUJWA) and Kuntas (HCUA) cited above or between Idnan and certain other Tuareg (MNLA) and Songhai (MUJWA).[22]

The state has to negotiate with the rebel groups nonetheless, primarily for two reasons. One is that they retain enough military capacity and political clout to perpetuate insecurity and act as spoilers of any peace agreement. Another is that, like the elected officials and the traditional chiefs, they appear to represent *some* northerners, even if they represent far fewer than they claim. There is therefore a strong incentive to involve as many armed groups as possible and include them in agreements—and these groups do strive to coordinate and speak as one, with mixed success—while keeping in mind that they do not speak for the entirety of the northern population. Negotiated agreements with them are necessary but not sufficient for establishing durable peace.

In the rest of this section, we briefly discuss each armed group with an eye toward understanding their representativeness. It is our central hypothesis that, although none is nearly as representative as each claims, each is sufficiently representative to merit inclusion. What complicates matters is that there is probably some truth to accusations of ties between different groups and criminal elements. It would be wrong, however, to reduce them to that.

---

[22] Rémi Carayol, "Mali: Le martyre de Gao," *Jeune Afrique*, February 25, 2013a; Dorothée Thienot, "Mali: Des patrouilleurs pour remplacer l'Etat à Gao," *Slate Afrique*, January 17, 2013; Hamma Biamoye, "'Nous pas bouger,' le mouvement de résistance de la jeunesse de Gao qui a fait le choix des islamistes," *Les observateurs*, July 9, 2012.

The National Movement for the Liberation of Azawad

The origins and aims of the MNLA have been well documented else-where.[23] The organization falsely boasts broad representativeness. How-ever, it does represent some important constituencies and is more than simply a vehicle for one or a few clans to advance their own narrow interests.

MNLA membership derives primarily from Kel Adagh Tuareg, as is frequently noted, but its leadership hails predominantly from a specific clan within the Kel Adagh confederation, the Idnan, who are peripheral to the noble clans at the core of the confederation (with whom they have ambiguous and complex relations) and have demon-strated a will to advance their relative position and assert themselves.[24] Others have joined the MNLA or otherwise support it—e.g., Imghad Tuareg, Chemenammas Tuareg, Songhai, Arabs—although exact numbers or proportions are impossible to come by. Many Tuareg, pos-sibly a majority, are opposed to the MNLA for a variety of reasons—in particular, members of tribal confederations other than the Kel Adagh, such as the Kel Ansar and the Kel Iwellemmedan. Thus a prominent Kel Antsar and former high-level Malian government official asserts that Tuareg want nothing to do with the MNLA and blames the rebel-lion on Kidal Tuareg (i.e., Kel Adagh Tuareg) and their internal strug-gles: "The rebellion is always Kidal and always ends in Kidal."[25] Others who are opposed to the MNLA, however, express a measure of soli-darity with it, at least to the extent that they recognize the validity of some of the MNLA's claims without sharing its agenda. According to an Arab leader interviewed for this study, except for the insistence on independence, most of the MNLA's grievances are "shared by others."[26] However, he, like many others, resents the MNLA for appropriating

---

[23] See, for example, Eric Wulf and Farley Mesko, *Guide to a Post-Conflict Mali*, Washington, D.C.: C4ADS, 2013, pp. 33–41; International Crisis Group, 2012, pp. 8, 11–14.

[24] Rida Lyammouri, "Understanding Who's Who in Northern Mali: Terrorists Secession-ists and Criminals," panel presentation, Johns Hopkins University School of Advanced International Studies, Washington, D.C., March 11, 2013.

[25] Tuareg leader and former high-level Malian government official, 2013.

[26] Arab leader A, 2013.

for itself the right to speak for the north. Most, it seems, agree that, notwithstanding the group's limitations, "one has to include them."[27] The group itself experienced internal tensions from the beginning, between staunch supporters of Azawad independence and those who preferred some form of autonomy akin to what could be found in a federal state and between those who were ready to find an agreement with the jihadists of Ansar Dine and those who considered secularism to be nonnegotiable.

The High Council for the Unity of Azawad

The HCUA is arguably the most transparent of militant groups in northern Mali in that it clearly represents the interests of the family of the Kel Adagh amenokal, elite Kel Adagh clans, and those who support the historical hierarchy, most notably the traditional chief of the Kuntas, Baba Ould Sidi El Moctar.[28] The HCUA is more of a political than armed group, one that is anxious to distinguish itself post-Serval from the MNLA and, above all, Ansar Dine. Ansar Dine drew the core of its leadership and support from many of the same Kel Adagh elites as the HCUA; however, Ansar Dine was an explicitly Islamist organization aligned with AQIM,[29] and it appears to have shattered after contact with the French military in January 2013. The amenokal's son, Alghabass Ag Intalla, had served as Iyad Ag Ghaly's deputy in Ansar Dine but broke with the group just days after Serval began. Alghabass Ag Intalla named his group the Mouvement islamique de l'Azawad (MIA), stating that he favored peace and disavowed extremism. MIA

---

[27] Berabiche leader, 2013.

[28] Wulf and Mesko, 2013, p. 42; Berabiche leader, 2013.

[29] This report does not examine in detail AQIM, which has been studied in depth elsewhere. See, for instance, Jean-Pierre Filiu, *Could Al-Qaeda Turn African in the Sahel?* Washington, D.C.: Carnegie Endowment for International Peace, June 10, 2010; Adib Benchérif, "Résilience d'Al-Qaïda au Maghreb islamique au nord du Mali," *Réflexion*, November 12, 2013; Geoff D. Porter, "AQIM's Objectives in North Africa," *CTC Sentinel*, Vol. 4, No. 2, February 2011, pp. 5–8; Christopher S. Chivvis and Andrew Liepman, *North Africa's Menace: AQIM's Evolution and the U.S. Policy Response*, Santa Monica, Calif.: RAND Corporation, RR-415-OSD, 2013.

dissolved in May 2013 to become the HCUA.[30] Its secretary general is Alghabass Ag Intalla's brother, Mohamed Ag Intalla, and its president is none other than Alghabass Ag Intalla's father, the amenokal Intalla Ag Attaher.

The HCUA's ties to Ansar Dine, as well as the narrow ethnic focus of its leadership, certainly diminish it in the eyes of some.[31] However, it is hard to imagine crafting a durable peace without the Kel Adagh elites or in opposition to them. A Berabiche leader made the case succinctly:

> One cannot isolate the family of Intalla. They count. They are going to continue to count. It's better to have them with one than be without them, and besides, one remembers how AQIM evolved. [The Intalla family] were the closest to [AQIM]. They did it to protect themselves against the others. As for the ideological and Islamic dimension, the Tuareg nobles and the Berabiches and Kuntas can . . . be extremists [only] as an adaptation strategy. They found themselves in the position of feeling obliged to join.[32]

Although the Kel Adagh elites have been the spoilers of every past peace agreement, they cannot be ignored, if only because of their potential to cause further harm if they feel threatened. Some members of the Kel Adagh, for instance, showed a willingness to treat with Islamists and AQIM if they found that doing so could be to their political advantage. The Kel Adagh can also at times prove helpful, if only because they represent a very heterogeneous group, as evidenced by the rift between the amenokal, who publicly supported the MNLA, and his son Alghabass Ag Intalla, who had a leading position in Ansar Dine.

---

[30] Wulf and Mesko, 2013, p. 42; "Mali: Des membres d'Ansar Dine font sécession et créent leur propre mouvement," *Radio France internationale*, January 24, 2013.

[31] Wulf and Mesko, 2013, p. 43.

[32] Berabiche leader, 2013.

The Arab Movement of Azawad

The MAA's origins are less well known that those of the MNLA and are tied to the events immediately preceding and following the takeover in Timbuktu by the MNLA and later Islamist groups in April 2012. According to Wulf and Mesko, wealthy Arab notables—businesspeople and traffickers—resisted the MNLA's entry into the city but allowed AQIM to enter; AQIM then pushed the Arabs out, prompting Meydou (who had led an Arab rebel group in the 1990s and who joined Gamou in 2008 in combating a rebel Tuareg bastion) to organize the Front de libération nationale de l'Azawad (FNLA), a militia combining Berabiche and Kunta communities.[33] The FNLA quickly evolved into the MAA under slightly different leadership because, according to Wulf and Mesko, of criticism that FNLA collaborated with AQIM.

The MAA has strong ties to prominent Arab businesspeople with unsavory connections to trafficking networks, many of which allegedly have grown with the willing complicity of Malian government officials.[34] These ties have enabled the MAA's critics to condemn it as little more than the instrument of state-abetted criminal interests. In what is likely a rather simplistic description, a Berabiche notable, for example, paints the MAA as being at the service of traffickers and organized by ATT, who used it to divide communities and pit them against one another.[35]

Nonetheless, it appears that the MAA, like the MNLA, has support within several Arab communities (including Berabiche and Kuntas) that goes beyond illicit interests. Moreover, the MAA, unlike the MNLA, does not aspire to independence and in fact is not a rebel group in the sense that it does not regard itself as at war with the Malian state. On the contrary, it should be seen more as an effort to protect Arab interests and to ensure that Arab communities have a proverbial seat at the table, lest they be squeezed out by more-aggressive Tuareg groups who tend to attract the most attention and solicitude. It is important to remember that some Arabs have been forcibly expelled from villages

---

[33] Wulf and Mesko, 2013, p. 47; Grémont, 2010b, p. 21.

[34] Wulf and Mesko, 2013, p. 48.

[35] Berabiche leader, 2013.

in the Timbuktu and Gao regions because they were accused of collaborating with the 2012 MUJWA/AQIM "occupation"—or because locals seized an opportunity to retaliate against powerful commercial operators.[36] That said, some sources have indicated that the MAA is itself split, with one faction siding with the MNLA and negotiating along with it and another with Mali and the Ganda Koy.[37]

The Patriotic Resistance Forces

The Patriotic Resistance Forces (Forces patriotiques de résistance, or FPR) is an umbrella group that consists of elements from the Ganda Koy and Ganda Iso, which were Songhai and Fulani self-defense militias that have clashed with Tuareg and were involved in attacks on Tuareg and Arab civilians during the 1990s. The Ganda Koy were allegedly created by the Malian government in 1994, although Lecocq's account makes clear that, regardless of the involvement of Songhai military officers, the movement emerged as a spontaneous response to insecurity that threatened the life and property of Songhai populations, as well as concern that Arabs and Tuareg, by rebelling, were advancing their own interests to the exclusion of the Songhais'.[38] The movement's reemergence in recent years underscores the relevance of these complaints—namely, insecurity and concern that the interests of the Songhai community were ignored as Arabs and Tuareg fought and negotiated with Bamako.

---

[36] Sahel expert D, written correspondence with Stephanie Pezard, September 3, 2014.

[37] Arab leader B, 2013; Berabiche leader, 2013.

[38] Lecocq, 2010, pp. 336–353.

CHAPTER FIVE

Is There a Nigerien Model of Resilience?

Since 2012, as Mali was facing near state collapse, Niger has appeared relatively stable, sufficiently so to serve as a centerpiece of the U.S. and French defense posture in the Sahel. (For a map of Niger's position in the region, see Figure 5.1.) Not only did Niger send troops to serve in the African-Led International Support Mission in Mali (AFISMA), followed by MINUSMA; it also welcomed U.S. and French military forces on its territory to operate surveillance aircraft. As a result, Niger played a critical role in Operation Serval in Mali and now forms a pillar of both nations' counterterrorism efforts in the region. The divergence of fates between Niger and Mali is especially puzzling because they share numerous factors of instability, from weak governance and pervasive poverty to a legacy of northern rebellions and military coups. Both countries were also exposed to similar external shocks when the Qadhafi regime collapsed in Libya, triggering the return of thousands of Nigeriens and Malians with little hope of being integrated into strained local economies.[1] Some of these returnees brought back not only military experience gained in Qadhafi's wars but also weapons looted from his arsenals. Still, Niger did not experience a renewed Tuareg rebellion like Mali did in 2011, and its military ostensibly remained under the control of civilian authorities.

This section explores three hypotheses that could explain why Niger remained stable while Mali was collapsing. The first one highlights structural factors and examines whether Niger was more solid

---

[1] Although it is worth noting that Niger had more civilians return from Libya, whereas Mali had more ex-combatants (Sahel expert D, 2014).

Figure 5.1
Map of Niger

SOURCE: Central Intelligence Agency, "Niger," last updated June 20, 2014b.
RAND *RR892-5.1*

than Mali to begin with. Do Niger's political institutions, its economy, and its political culture contain elements that make Niger more resilient than Mali? A second hypothesis focuses on contextual factors. Should Niger's enduring stability be credited to the policies of President Mahamadou Issoufou and his predecessor, Mamadou Tandja, which emphasized both security and development and contrasted sharply with the laissez-faire approach that prevailed under ATT's reign in Mali? A third hypothesis cannot be dispelled. Niger might have simply been lucky. In other words, Niger is arguably still fragile—especially as the Libyan and Malian crises have failed to recede entirely—and risks experiencing a major crisis in the short to medium term. This last hypothesis highlights the shortcomings of the Nigerien model of northern integration and the security threats that remain.

Understanding why Niger managed at the very least to avoid the worst in 2012 is important for three reasons. First, it might provide an indication of whether Niger's stability can be expected to last. This question is all the more important now that the United States and France have sizable military presences in the country and are, in effect, counting on Niger to remain a viable partner. Second, the numerous similarities between the political, economic, and social contexts of Niger and Mali suggest that any positive lesson from Niger could benefit Mali and help in rebuilding the latter on sounder bases. These lessons will be particularly useful as Mali's Western partners rethink what type of assistance they want to provide to this country without risking seeing their resources wasted or, worse, misused once again. Third, the Nigerien case could provide insights as to what Mali can expect in the future. One particular issue to monitor closely is the role of Niger's extractive industry, uranium mining. Did it bring instability, in a classic case of resource curse?[2] Or did it give instead all political actors a stake in security and the revenues that flow from it? The answer matters for Mali—and, to some extent, other countries in the region, such as Mauritania—as the oil-rich Taoudeni basin extends over their territories. Although Mali is still at the exploration phase for hydrocarbons in the north,[3] the location of these resources in the north might create more challenges (by encouraging separatist claims) or opportu-

---

[2]   The term *resource curse* summarizes a paradox—namely, that countries with plentiful natural resources tend to experience more economic and development problems than countries with fewer resources, for several reasons, ranging from increased corruption of governmental institutions to the capture of all investments by resource-extraction industries to the crowding out of other sectors (see, for instance, Richard M. Auty, *Sustaining Development in Mineral Economies: The Resource Curse Thesis*, London: Routledge, 1993; Jeffrey D. Sachs and Andrew M. Warner, "The Curse of Natural Resources," *European Economic Review*, Vol. 45, 2001, pp. 827–838).

[3]   Aïda Haddad, "Maroc-Mali: Renforcement du partenariat dans les mines et les hydrocarbures," *Le point*, May 14, 2014.

nities (by providing locals with some of the resources that Bamako has not yet been able or willing to channel toward its most-impoverished regions).

Overall, the Nigerien experience suggests that, in spite of the differences that exist between the two countries, Mali can learn from some of the factors that have kept Niger stable so far. A key one is promoting the integration of minority communities, particularly Tuareg. Niger also shows an example of a lesser north–south divide, which Mali can emulate to some extent by improving basic services and the transport infrastructure that will, over time, promote economic development in the north and encourage geographic mobility across its territory. Finally, Niger's recent efforts in favor of development suggest that such programs are a promising step toward reducing risks of radicalization, even though they have yet to deliver on many of their promises.

Mali and Niger: Two Very Similar Neighbors

Structural Similarities

Niger and Mali have numerous characteristics in common, as highlighted in Table 5.1. Located on the Sahelian belt, both are former French colonies that became independent in 1960. They share low levels of human development, saw decades of autocratic rule before converting to democracy, experienced multiple military coups against civilian and military leaders, and deal with a problematic north–south divide, with the former suffering from a lack of economic opportunities, basic services, and infrastructures. The road between the capital city, Niamey, and the main urban center in the northern part of the country, Agadez, is reportedly in worse condition today than it was 20 years ago.[4]

Niger and Mali share additional challenges. Each country is landlocked, shares borders with seven others, and is at a crossroads of trafficking routes. Concerns that terrorist groups could use their territo-

---

[4] Rémi Carayol, "Niger: Le pays où les Touaregs bénéficient de la décentralisation," *Jeune Afrique*, May 22, 2013c.

Table 5.1
A Comparison of Mali's and Niger's Socioeconomic Indicators

Indicator	Mali	Niger
Population size (millions of people)[a]	15.3	17.83
Recent democratic transition	1992	1993
Low human development (rank out of 187 countries, with higher numbers being worse)[b]	176	187
Recurrent military coups[c]	1968, 1991, 2012	1974, 1996, 1999, 2010
Strong demographic expansion (annual population growth rate, %)[d]	2.8	3.6
Rapid increase of urban population (average annual growth rate of urban population, %)[d]	4.8	4.3
Young population (median age, years)[b]	16.17	14.96
Short life expectancy (years)[e]	54.6	57.9

[a] UN Development Programme (UNDP), *Sustaining Human Progress: Reducing Vulnerabilities and Building Resilience*, New York, July 2014.

[b] UNDP, 2014.

[c] Successful military coups since independence.

[d] Calculated for 1990 to 2012. UN Children's Fund (UNICEF), "Country Statistics," updated May 8, 2003.

[e] UNICEF, 2003.

ries as a base have led the United States to incorporate them in its Pan Sahel Initiative and the subsequent Trans-Sahara Counterterrorism Partnership. Terrorist attacks on Nigerien soil since 2008 show that AQIM and, more recently, MUJWA have been active in Niger. These attacks include the kidnapping of foreigners and suicide bombings, most recently against Army barracks in Agadez and a uranium mine in Arlit in May 2013. The Adrar des Ifoghas, a mountainous area of Mali whose geologic features make it an ideal hideout for criminal and terrorist groups, even has an extension in Niger in the Aïr region.[5]

Niger's history of northern populations perceiving themselves as disenfranchised echoes Mali's. The French colonial administration

---

[5] Keita, 2002; Rémi Carayol, "Niger, au milieu du chaos," *Jeune Afrique*, April 24, 2013b.

favored Djerma (the second-largest group in Niger, after the Hausa) over nomadic populations in terms of education and political access, as they did with the Bambara in Mali.[6] This, in addition to the Tuareg's proportionately lower participation in French colonial education, resulted in Djermas and Bambara being promoted as the administrative elite of their respective countries and taking over political institutions at the time of independence.[7] Whether in Niger or Mali, nomadic populations also experienced the same dramatic droughts in the 1970s and 1980s, which led their members to emigrate en masse toward Libya—while those they left behind started to feel disenfranchised by states they felt were not helping them.[8] This negative perception of the government in Niamey was made worse by the repression that followed the participation of several Tuareg officers in a coup attempt against President Seyni Kountché in 1976, Libyan-sponsored radicalization of those Tuareg who had left Niger, and the disastrous experience of the tens of thousands of returnees who came back to Niger following President Ali Saibou's call in 1990 but did not find economic opportunities or support that would have allowed them to reintegrate into Nigerien life.[9] All these elements provide the background for the Tuareg rebellion that started in May 1990 in Niger before spreading to Mali.[10]

Initially, the Aïr and Azawak Liberation Front (Front de libération de l'Aïr et de l'Azawak [FLAA]) led the rebellion in Niger.[11] As in Mali, Tuareg are an extremely divided community, with a similar

---

[6] International Crisis Group, *Niger: Another Weak Link in the Sahel?* Brussels, Africa Report 208, September 19, 2013, p. 5

[7] Yvan Guichaoua, *Circumstantial Alliances and Loose Loyalties in Rebellion Making: The Case of Tuareg Insurgency in Northern Niger (2007–2009)*, A Micro Level Analysis of Violent Conflict Research Working Paper 20, December 2009, p. 8; Sahel expert B, phone interview with Stephanie Pezard, April 22, 2014.

[8] International Crisis Group, 2013, pp. 8–9.

[9] International Crisis Group, 2013, pp. 9, 11; David Lea and Annamarie Rowe, eds., *A Political Chronology of Africa*, London: Europa Publications, 2001, p. 330; André Salifou, *La question touarègue au Niger*, Paris: Karthala, 1993, pp. 48–51; Claudot-Hawad, 1996, pp. 39, 41

[10] International Crisis Group, 2013, p. 11; Raffray, 2013, p. 51; Keita, 2002.

[11] International Crisis Group, 2013, pp. 11–12.

system of clans and confederations.[12] As a result, the FLAA quickly fractured into more armed groups asking for increased autonomy for the northern region and for more political and administrative power at the local level.[13] As in Mali, the rebellion spurred the creation, by and in support of the government, of militias from sedentary populations.[14] This rebellion lasted five years and ended with the Ouagadougou Accord signed in 1995 with all armed groups.[15] The content of this accord was similar to what Malian groups had obtained through the 1991 Tamanrasset Accord and the 1992 National Pact: the beginning of a decentralization process, integration of former combatants into national security forces and administration, and more resources for the development of the north.[16]

As in Mali, former members of armed groups soon became disillusioned with the degree of implementation of the accord. In 2007, one year after Mali went through a new, albeit short-lived, rebellion, the Niger Movement for Justice (Mouvement des Nigériens pour la justice [MNJ]) led by former FLAA leader Aghaly Ag Alambo attacked the town of Iferouane near Agadez. The grievances voiced by the MNJ had changed little since the 1990s: The group called for more resources for the north, more development, and better redistribution of the country's revenues. The redistribution issue was complicated by the fact that an important source of revenue for the country is uranium, which is being exploited in the north of the country.[17] The MNJ asked for more mining-related jobs for the local population and a larger share of mining

---

[12] Sahel expert B, 2014.

[13] International Crisis Group, 2013, p. 11.

[14] International Crisis Group, 2013, p. 12.

[15] For a more elaborate history of the Tuareg rebellion in Niger in the 1990s, see Emmanuel Grégoire, *Touaregs du Niger, le destin d'un mythe*, new ed., Paris: Karthala, 2010; Frédéric Deycard, *Les rébellions touarègues du Niger: Combattants, mobilisation et culture politique*, Institut d'études politiques de Bordeaux, doctoral thesis, January 12, 2011. For an abbreviated account of these events, see Raffray, 2013, pp. 51–62.

[16] International Crisis Group, 2013, p. 12.

[17] Stratfor, "Niger: A Rebel Threat to the Uranium Sector," Austin, Texas, February 1, 2008.

revenue for local communities.[18] The MNJ's rebellion eventually faltered in the face of Tandja's no-concessions policy and because, unlike in the 1990s, it could never muster sufficient popular support.[19]

Similar External Shocks

Beyond these structural similarities, Mali and Niger also experienced a similar crisis with the fall of Libyan leader Muammar Qadhafi in 2011 and its impact across the region. Between 80,000 and 160,000 Nigeriens, depending on estimates, returned from Libya to their home country.[20] Some had been employed in Qadhafi's military or personal guard and brought back large numbers of weapons.[21] Many of these returnees spent what little they had to pay for the trip back to Niger, and they were going back to communities that could hardly offer them opportunities to make a living, having themselves largely survived on remittances until the fall of Libya, and were, at the time, facing a regional drought.[22] In 2011, a journalist noted that "some 86% of the returning migrant workers support five family members or more, in a region where food security is precarious."[23] Niger not only had to absorb these

---

[18] International Crisis Group, 2013, p. 13, note 78.

[19] International Crisis Group, 2013, p. 14.

[20] According to aid agencies, 80,000 (Rosa Wild, "Security and Insecurity in Niger," *Think Africa Press*, November 11, 2011); according to the International Crisis Group, 90,000 (International Crisis Group, 2013, p. 37); 160,000 according to Issoufou when interviewed for *Radio France internationale* (Boubacar Guede, "Niger: Le président Issoufou lance un appel aux rebelles maliens," *Radio France internationale*, February 14, 2012).

[21] Charlotte Bozonnet, "Niger Remains Wary of Mali Crisis on Its Doorstep," *Guardian*, March 5, 2013.

[22] Wild, 2011; Peter Tinti, "Niger: The Stable Sahelian State, for Now," *Think Africa Press*, September 27, 2013. For more details on Libyan returnees in the Sahel region, see Asmita Naik, *Returnees from Libya: The Bittersweet Experience of Coming Home*, Geneva: International Organization for Migration, Policy in Brief, May 2012; United Nations Security Council, *Report of the Assessment Mission on the Impact of the Libyan Crisis on the Sahel Region, 7 to 23 December 2011*, New York, S/2012/42, January 18, 2012.

[23] Wild, 2011.

returnees but also was under pressure at the time to provide for refugees from other countries, including Ivory Coast and, soon, Mali.[24]

Three Hypotheses to Explain Niger's Resilience

Given these similarities and context, Niger seemed at least as likely as Mali to experience political and social turmoil. Yet, it remained stable while its neighbor experienced a Tuareg rebellion, an Islamist takeover of its northern part, and a military coup. This section examines three potential explanations for Niger's resilience.

First Hypothesis: Niger Is Structurally More Solid Than Mali

A first set of potential explanations for this remarkable stability is the possibility that, in spite of its many commonalities with Mali, Niger might have some structural factors that make it more resistant to external and internal shocks—be they infiltration by Islamist groups, a large influx of returnees, or brewing political or military discontent—or more capable of absorbing them.

A key element of resilience might be found in Niger's population, which happens to be more mixed geographically than Mali's.[25] As a result, even though Niger's Tuareg population is proportionally larger than Mali's (10 percent and 3.5 percent of the overall population, respectively)[26] and is concentrated in the northern part of the country like Mali's is, there is no equivalent in Niger of Kidal, where Tuareg represent a large majority of the town's population. Nigerien Tuareg's

---

[24] Tinti, 2013; Guede, 2012.

[25] International Crisis Group, 2013, p. 30; Sahel expert C, phone interview with Stephanie Pezard, April 24, 2014.

[26] Carayol, 2013c. The figure of 10 percent is also found in Bozonnet, 2013. The figure for Mali is an approximation based on the number of respondents who stated that Tamasheq was their mother tongue in the 2009 population census (Seydou Moussa Traore, Assa Gakou Doumbia, Vinima Traore, and Daniel Fassa Tolno, *4ème recensement général de la population et de l'habitat du Mali (RPGH-2009): Analyse des résultats définitifs*, Thème 2: *État et structure de la population*, République du Mali, Ministère de l'économie et des finances, Institut national de la statistique, Bureau central du recensement, December 2011, p. 75).

greater integration into multi-ethnic communities could explain why independence claims have found less of an echo in Niger than in Mali. Niger also seems to experience a less dramatic north–south divide than Mali does.[27] For instance, Agadez is more accessible from the capital Niamey than Gao is from Bamako because the travel time for the former is about a one-day drive and the latter requires a three-day drive.[28]

Niger might have been protected from the contagion of rebellions by the fact that its Tuareg have historically showed selective solidarity of action with their Malian counterparts. Cross-border contagion certainly happened a few times: As mentioned above, the 1990 Niger rebellion marked the start of the Tuareg uprising in Mali. In 2007, too, some Nigerien Tuareg were involved in the first attack carried out by Bahanga's ATNM, a Malian group whose name reflects its pan-Tuareg nature or, at the very least, its pan-Tuareg ambitions. In a media interview, Bahanga highlighted the similarities of issues faced by Tuareg in Mali and Niger and claimed that the ATNM's military alliance with the MNJ would soon be followed by a political one.[29] This alliance, however, was short-lived. The MNJ soon denied any involvement in the ATNM's fight.[30] Overall, their cooperation seems to have been limited to providing each other with logistical support and a rear base; they might also have relied on each other to move hostages between the two countries.[31] The MNJ's agenda was largely focused on the national, rather than regional, level. Overall, contrary to Bahanga's claims, Tuareg in Mali and Niger "are different communities, with different demographic, political and historical relationships with their

---

[27] International Crisis Group, 2013, p. 30; Sahel expert C, 2014.

[28] Sahel expert C, 2014.

[29] Bahanga quoted in "Interview de Ibrahim Bahanga: 'L'alliance entre le MNJ et nous existe depuis que nous avons reçu des formations militaires en Libye,'" *L'indépendant* (Bamako), August 30, 2007. Author's translation.

[30] Integrated Regional Information Networks, "Mali: Indignation Dominates Reaction as Attacks in North Escalate," August 31, 2007.

[31] Malian journalist, phone interview with Stephanie Pezard, August 2009.

respective governments."[32] In spite of warnings that international intervention in the 2012 Malian rebellion could result in a mobilization of Tuareg from neighboring countries, no such solidarity emerged, and only small numbers of Nigerien Tuareg joined the MNLA.[33]

This lack of systematic solidarity of Nigerien and Malian Tuareg might be due to Niger's history of integrating Tuareg more thoroughly into political, administrative, and military institutions. Tuareg were already present in the first governments of Niger following independence.[34] This early integration might explain in part why Niger, unlike Mali, did not experience a Tuareg rebellion in the 1960s. This practice has endured over the years. In April 2011, Issoufou chose Brigi Rafini, a Tuareg, as prime minister, only the second time that this has happened since Kountché chose Hamid Algabid to be prime minister from 1983 to 1988.[35] As of early 2014, other high-level Tuareg officials included the foreign minister's chief of staff, the prime minister's deputy chief of staff, and the deputy chair of the joint chiefs of staff.[36] The High Authority for Peacebuilding (Haute autorité à la consolidation de la paix, formerly Haut commissariat à la restauration de la paix) has been headed by former leader of the Union of the Forces of Armed Resistance (Union des forces de la résistance armée [UFRA]) Anacko and Colonel Mahamadou Abou Tarka, both Tuareg.[37] Nige-

[32] Tinti, 2013.

[33] See, for instance, former Nigerien Tuareg rebel leader Mohamed Anacko cited in Grégoire, 2013, p. 9; International Crisis Group, 2013, p. 33.

[34] International Crisis Group, 2013, p. 6.

[35] Anne Kappès-Grangé, "Niger: Le Premier ministre Brigi Rafini, en toute discrétion," *Jeune Afrique*, November 7, 2011. As a comparison, Mali has had only one Tuareg prime minister, Hamani, who held this position from 2002 to 2004. Several other prime ministers came from northern Mali, however. Cissé Mariam Kaïdama Sidibé, prime minister in 2011 and 2012, for instance, was born in Timbuktu. Ousmane Issoufi Maïga, prime minister from 2004 to 2007, was born in the Gao region.

[36] International Crisis Group, 2013, p. 31.

[37] Carayol, 2013c.

rien Tuareg also seem better integrated into the economic realm than their Malian counterparts.[38]

The decentralization process that was instituted following the Ouagadougou Accord has also played a role in putting more members of minority (i.e., non-Djerma and non-Hausa) communities in positions of power, including several prominent former members of Tuareg armed groups. A majority of mayors in the Agadez region are Tuareg.[39] Anacko is the president of the Regional Council for Agadez; former leaders of the MNJ Rhissa Feltou and Issouf Ag Maha have become mayor of Agadez and mayor of Tchirozérine (north of Agadez), respectively.[40] Niger's policy was to adopt a hardline stance against Tuareg combatants during the 2007 rebellion, refusing to negotiate with what the government called "bandits" and "terrorists," but to pursue a long-term policy of reconciliation and dialogue after the rebellion's military defeat and subsequent peace accords. As of 2012, three years after the end of the rebellion, the Nigerien government was still organizing "peace fora" where government officials, civil society representatives, and former rebels could meet.[41]

In the military, the Nigerien army has been mixing communities within its contingents, albeit amid continued Djerma dominance.[42] Some challenges remain, however. The International Crisis Group cites cases of Tuareg who integrated into the Nigerien forces after the peace accords in the 1990s but left after feeling that they were not promoted as quickly as others.[43] These stories contrast with the highly publicized achievements of some other Tuareg, such as the current deputy chair of the joint chiefs of staff. On this issue, it is difficult to establish which

---

[38] Roland Marchal, "The Coup in Mali: The Result of a Long-Term Crisis or Spillover from the Libyan Civil War?" Oslo: Norwegian Peacebuilding Resource Centre, May 2012, p. 6.

[39] International Crisis Group, 2013, p. 31, note 176.

[40] Mathieu Pellerin, "La résilience nigérienne à l'épreuve de la guerre au Mali," *L'Afrique en questions*, No. 15, Institut français de relations internationales, February 2013.

[41] International Crisis Group, 2013, p. 31, note 176; Emmanuel Grégoire, "Islamistes et rebelles touaregs maliens: Alliances, rivalités et ruptures," *Sur le vif*, July 3, 2013, p. 10.

[42] Sahel expert D, 2014.

[43] International Crisis Group, 2013, p. 19, note 123.

of the two types of stories is most typical and to compare the success of Tuareg integration in the armed forces between Niger and Mali. It is also worth noting that, in Niger as in Mali, there are still some tensions between civilians and the Army due to the memory of abuses committed by the latter.[44]

An assessment of the impact of these efforts toward Tuareg integration into state institutions and the economy is made all the more difficult by the fact that Niamey tends to overstate its achievements and the level of national unity prevailing in the country. Journalist Peter Tinti notes that "many Nigeriens scoff at the idea that the government in Niamey has made significant strides in integrating populations who feel marginalized. By some accounts, entire communities in northern Niger are still traumatized by the events in 2007."[45] Analyst Andrew Lebovich too underscores that some former Tuareg combatants see the appointment of prominent Tuareg officials as a superficial change that does not benefit them.[46] The International Crisis Group casts doubts on Rafini's actual powers as prime minister, noting that some of his ministers might be out of his control.[47] Finally, the political integration of minority communities, which builds national unity, also comes at a price because it might, in some cases, promote ethnic tokenism over competence.[48]

Niger's ability to integrate Tuareg into its society more effectively might also depend on institutions that are, overall, healthier than Mali's.[49] The 2013 edition of the Corruption Perceptions Index gives Mali a rank of 122 out of 177 countries (1 being the least corrupt, 177

---

[44] On abuses against civilians committed by the Nigerien army and the MNJ during the 2007 rebellion, see Human Rights Watch, "Niger: Warring Sides Must End Abuses of Civilians," December 20, 2007.

[45] Tinti, 2013.

[46] Andrew Lebovich, "Overstating Terror in Niger: Letter from Niamey," *Foreign Affairs*, August 14, 2013.

[47] International Crisis Group, 2013, p. 20.

[48] International Crisis Group, 2013, p. 6.

[49] Grégoire, 2013, p. 10.

the most), while Niger's rank is 106.[50] One reason for these lower corruption levels could be the fact that Niger, in spite of being on several key trafficking routes, does not seem to be as major a hub for drug trafficking as Mali is.[51] The UN Office on Drugs and Crime mentioned Mali, but not Niger, as a transit point for heroin and amphetamine-type stimulants.[52] Only limited amounts of cocaine have been seized in Niger relative to other West African countries, particularly Mali, where reports of cocaine being transported by the ton between South America and the north of the country have made the headlines since 2009.[53] This exceptional situation might not last, however, because some of the Malian traffic could seek to relocate to Niger while French and international troops are active in the country, and the Libyan power vacuum creates more criminal opportunities on Niger's eastern front.[54]

Finally, the role of France needs to be underlined. Because of the major mining interests it holds in Niger, France might have worked as a protective factor against a collapse of the state, as occurred in Mali. The French state controls 80 percent of the global mining company AREVA, which exploits the two main uranium mines in Niger near Arlit, north of Agadez.[55] Niger is the second-largest source of uranium for AREVA, and its uranium is used by more than 30 percent of French nuclear reactors, giving the country strategic weight for France, where

---

[50] Transparency International, "Corruption Perceptions Index 2013," undated (b); referenced April 2014.

[51] Grégoire, 2013, p. 10.

[52] United Nations Office on Drugs and Crime, *World Drug Report, 2013*, New York, May 2013, pp. 34, 56.

[53] Boris Thiolay, "Mali: La guerre de la cocaïne," *L'express*, March 21, 2013; Georges Berghezan, *Panorama du trafic de cocaïne en Afrique de l'ouest*, Brussels: Groupe de Recherche et d'Information sur la Paix et la Sécurité, June 1, 2012, p. 30.

[54] Berghezan, 2012, p. 31.

[55] "Accord stratégique entre le Niger et Areva sur les mines d'uranium," *Liberation*, May 26, 2014.

nuclear energy accounts for 75 percent of electricity produced.[56] As a result, France has supported Niger's border-security operations and sent special forces to reinforce the security of its mining sites in the wake of Operation Serval.[57] According to French expert on Niger Emmanuel Grégoire, this strategic importance of Nigerien uranium for France contributed to deterring Islamists from choosing Niger as a main operating base or attempting any major destabilization of Nigerien power.[58] Alternatively, Niger's support to the U.S. and French defense posture in the Sahel could make it an attractive target for anti-Western jihadis in the future.[59]

The presence of uranium ore in Niger makes its situation different from Mali's in another way: It probably made decentralization efforts easier to implement and more successful because of the mining revenue that was available at the local level. In Mali, the lack of resources (either local or sent from Bamako) limited the actual power of local officials; Niger was relatively insulated from this problem.[60] From 2004 to 2011, revenues from the uranium extracted by AREVA grew 350 percent.[61] In May 2013, the Nigerien Mining Code was revised so that 15 percent will go to communes and regional councils.[62] The amount of resources that they will receive is likely to increase in the future because, in May 2014, after many months of negotiations with the Nigerien state, AREVA agreed to be subjected to a 2006 law that increases mining royalties from 5.5 percent to 12 percent.[63] It is important to note, how-

---

[56] Anne-Sophie Simpere and Ali Idrissa, *Niger: À qui profite l'uranium? L'enjeu de la renégociation des contrats miniers d'AREVA*, Oxfam, November 2013; Pierre Le Hir, "Réduire à 50% la part du nucléaire en France, crédible ou non?" *Le monde*, December 5, 2013.

[57] International Crisis Group, 2013, p. 24, note 136.

[58] Grégoire, 2013, p. 11.

[59] Sahel expert D, 2014.

[60] International Crisis Group, 2013, p. 33.

[61] Grégoire, 2013, p. 11.

[62] International Crisis Group, 2013, p. 33.

[63] See, for instance, Jennifer Lazuta, "Niger Signs Long-Delayed Uranium Deal with Areva," *Voice of America*, May 27, 2014; "Accord stratégique entre le Niger et Areva sur les mines d'uranium," 2014.

ever, that uranium ore exploitation also has numerous drawbacks for northern Niger, from high levels of pollution to perceived unfairness about the levels to which uranium-ore extraction benefits local populations economically.[64]

Second Hypothesis: Niger Implemented the Right Policies in the Face of the Libyan Collapse

A second hypothesis to explain Niger's resilience to Tuareg and Islamist militancy focuses on contextual rather than structural factors. Are the Nigerien government's policies responsible for the country's greater stability?

Issoufou's personality might have played a role to begin with. The Tuareg population sees Issoufou in a more favorable light than it does his predecessor, Tandja, whom the Tuareg community accused of having played a key role in the 1990 massacres of Tchintabaraden and the brutal 2007–2008 counterinsurgency and was generally considered to be anti-Tuareg. As a result, Tuareg's relations with the Nigerien state do not have the level of tensions they had under Tandja.[65]

Issoufou also took measures to mitigate the consequences that the Libyan crisis had for Niger. In response to the influx of returnees, he launched Operation Mali-Bero in 2011.[66] This operation sent military reinforcement from the Nigerien Armed Forces (Forces armées nigériennes [FAN]) to monitor the border, where Defense Minister Karidjo Mahamadou remembers there being "many skirmishes."[67] The FAN inspected returnees and claims to have confiscated weapons when needed. Members of the military deployed in border-control operations were given strong financial incentives: According to a Western military source cited by the International Crisis Group, their per diem was

---

[64] Sahel expert B, 2014; Simpere and Idrissa, 2013.

[65] Sahel expert B, 2014.

[66] Dalatou Malam Mamane, "Mission de l'Unité de Fusion et de Liaison (UFL) au Niger: La lutte contre le terrorisme plus que jamais engagée par les Forces de Défense et de Sécurité nigériennes," *Le Sahel*, No. 8306, April 3, 2012, p. 7.

[67] Cited in Bozonnet, 2013.

doubled in October 2012.[68] Security measures further increased after the MNLA rebellion broke out in Mali, with more members of the FAN sent to secure Niger's western border, as well as mining sites in the Arlit region.[69] Members of the French special forces who moved to Arlit after the terrorist attack on a gas facility near In Amenas in Algeria in January 2013 supported them in this mission.[70] The capital, Niamey, was also put under a heightened state of surveillance, with checkpoints around the city controlling and registering entries and exits.[71]

Although it is impossible to know how many weapons Niger managed to keep off its territory with this heightened security effort, it stands in stark contrast with Mali's apparent leniency in that regard.[72] However, Niger's policy might also have compounded the problem in Mali because those who could not make their way into Niger might have continued west. Operation Mali-Bero's contribution to security in Niger has also received some critics. Tinti notes, "sources in Niger suggest that Issoufou's government did little more than outsource the task [of disarming returnees] to local proxies, whose loyalty to the Nigerien state only goes so far as their political and economic interests align."[73] This raises the question of Niamey's ability to impose real order in the north, especially because it cannot easily confront the key individuals involved in trafficking or armed groups because of the local power they wield.[74] Niger's ability to control its territory should not be overstated either. After the simultaneous terrorist attacks against Nigerien military barracks and a French mining site in northern Niger in May 2013, the U.S. State Department underlined that the former, in particular,

---

[68] International Crisis Group, 2013, p. 23, note 132.

[69] Bozonnet, 2013; International Crisis Group, 2013, p. 38, note 213.

[70] Steven Erlanger, "France Is Increasing Security at Sites in Niger and at Home," *New York Times,* January 24, 2013; "Niger Suicide Bombers Target Areva Mine and Barracks," *BBC,* May 23, 2013.

[71] Olivier Fourt, "Le Niger, un 'point d'appui' opérationnel pour la France," *Radio France internationale,* last modified May 28, 2013; Carayol, 2013b.

[72] Marchal, 2012, p. 3.

[73] Tinti, 2013.

[74] Lebovich, 2013.

"demonstrated significant gaps in Niger's ability to detect threats and organize a coordinated response."[75]

Niger also adopted broader policies that aim to go beyond border control to tackle the development issues that are a root cause of insecurity. In October 2012, Rafini launched the Strategy for Development and Security (SDS).[76] Budgeted at $2 billion, the SDS is a five-year plan specifically targeting northern Niger to be funded in equal proportions by the Nigerien government and external donors.[77] Improved security (to include border security and a consolidated program against small arms and light weapons) is only one of its components. The three others are improved access of the population to economic opportunities, improved access of the population to basic social services, and improved local governance.[78] The second component on improved economic opportunities alone absorbs more than half of the entire program's anticipated budget.[79] Through the SDS, Niger is attempting to develop a policy that would focus both on security and development, in order to keep the most-dangerous individuals at bay and integrate economically those who came back to their communities of origin in the hope of thwarting inclinations toward rebellion or radicalization. Securing the north is also seen as a condition for attracting more employment-generating activities, such as tourism, creating a virtuous circle whereby economic activity would further reduce incentives to take arms.[80] The SDS is included in the larger framework of the Economic and Social Development Plan (Plan de développement

---

[75] U.S. Department of State, "Chapter 2: Country Reports—Africa Overview," in *Country Reports on Terrorism 2013*, April 2014, pp. 11–228.

[76] "Lancement au Niger d'une stratégie de développement et de sécurité," *Panapress*, October 2, 2012; Nigerien Prime Minister's Office, "Synthèse PAP SE/SDS Sahel-Niger," briefing, November 26, 2013.

[77] Lebovich, 2013.

[78] Nigerien Prime Minister's Office, 2013.

[79] Nigerien Prime Minister's Office, 2013.

[80] Laurent Touchard, "Niger: Les enjeux de la coopération sécuritaire avec la France," *Jeune Afrique*, March 3, 2014.

économique et social [PDES]), for which donors pledged $4.8 billion and which focuses on diversifying Niger's economic activities.[81]

As of mid-2014, progress made on the SDS or the PDES were still unclear. Their success was based on the optimistic assumption of strong growth rates based in part on increased exports in the mining industry.[82] The price of uranium, however, has been decreasing steadily since 2011 and the Fukushima disaster.[83] The new agreement signed between AREVA and the Nigerien state on May 26, 2014, indefinitely delays the exploitation of the new Imouraren site, on which the Nigerien government had been counting to increase its revenue.[84] Consequently, Niger will again depend critically on external donors to implement its ambitious programs and meet the expectations of its population, but actual delivery of donor aid might also be below pledges.[85]

Third Hypothesis: Niger Owes Its Survival to Luck

A third hypothesis should be examined: The elements described above might have played only a marginal role in Niger's ability to stay the course, and it might only be a matter of months or years before Niger, too, reverts to the civil unrest and military coups that have marked much of its past. In this perspective, Niger's stability would be only a lucky coincidence. The continued existence in Niger of numerous contributors to instability supports this pessimistic hypothesis. Some have been present for a long time, while others are more recent or are a direct consequence of the Libyan and Malian crises.

---

[81] UNDP, "In Paris, Niger Mobilizes $4.8 Billion for Development," November 16, 2012; "Mise en œuvre du PDES 2012–2015: Un instrument de référence pour impulser une mutation qualitative de l'économie nigérienne," *Le Sahel*, undated; referenced June 2014; Alex Thurston, "Niger Secures $4.8 Billion for Security and Development: Is This a Regional Model?" *Sahel Blog*, November 16, 2012b.

[82] "Mise en œuvre du PDES 2012–2015," undated.

[83] "5 Year Uranium Prices and Price Chart," *InvestmentMine*, undated; referenced June 2014; Véronique Le Billon, "Uranium: Areva et le Niger scellent un nouvel accord," *Les échos*, May 26, 2014; Christophe Boisbouvier, "Uranium: le Niger n'a 'rien à cacher' sur l'accord avec Areva," *Radio France internationale*, June 4, 2014.

[84] Boisbouvier, 2014.

[85] Sahel expert D, 2014.

Niger's political system remains fragile. There is no indication that civilian control of armed forces has improved. Relations between political and military powers are still uncomfortably close, and the latter could again decide to intervene on the political scene.[86] This almost happened in July 2011, when Issoufou reportedly foiled a coup attempt by the military.[87] This constant threat limits Issoufou's scope of action. Not only does he have to placate the members of the military who might have the ambition and sufficient clout to foment a coup; he also has to do the same with political opponents who might be tempted to create the kind of political blockages that have, in the past, prompted the military to intervene to "solve" the crisis.[88] Political tensions are frequent in Niger and have been increasing since August 2013, when president of the parliament, Hama Amadou, who is a potential adversary of Issoufou in the 2016 presidential election and left the government's majority coalition. A series of arrests of members of the opposition and journalists, as well as attacks against houses of members of the opposition and majority, occurred in the first half of 2014.[89] These events underline the inherent fragility of Nigerien democracy.

Another source of fragility for Nigerien civilian power is the fact that it has been relying, to a large extent, on a strategy similar to ATT's to placate potential troublemakers in the north.[90] This strategy has consisted of giving positions of power to key figures who can prevent the resurgence of violence.[91] Not only does this strategy risk

---

[86] International Crisis Group, 2013, pp. 22–23.

[87] Ibbo Abdoulaye, "10 Arrested in Niger Coup Attempt, President Says," *CNN*, August 3, 2011; "Au Niger, le président Issoufou dénonce une tentative de coup d'État," *Radio France internationale*, August 3, 2011; International Crisis Group, 2013, p. 23.

[88] Tinti, 2013; Niger expert, conversation with Stephanie Pezard, June 2014. The Niger expert underlined that, generally, political opposition has won the first elections following the handing back of power to civilians by the military.

[89] "Le Niger s'enfonce dans une crise politique," *Jeune Afrique*, June 5, 2014; "Des opposants arrêtés et un journal fermé au Niger," *Le monde*, May 25, 2014.

[90] The International Crisis Group highlights that a similar strategy by ATT has allowed local power brokers to control armed groups and trafficking routes in northern Mali (International Crisis Group, 2013, p. 36).

[91] International Crisis Group, 2013, p. 35.

creating an impression of impunity and weakness of the government; there are also limits to what it can achieve. Scholar Yvan Guichaoua notes, for instance, that, when the former leader of the FLAA, Rhissa Ag Boula, became minister of tourism in 1997 (he served in that role until 2004), he "was also implicitly given discretionary powers to prevent any insurrectional aspiration to resume in the Agadez region."[92] When Boula was sent to jail for suspected involvement in the murder of a local politician, "the FLAA was then re-formed temporarily to serve the interests of its chief,"[93] resulting in his rapid release. This suggests that powerful individuals and groups could easily remobilize if it became in their interest to do so.[94] The Nigerien political leadership is aware of this risk and has been acting accordingly. After former leader of the MNJ Alambo was arrested in March 2012 on terrorism charges, he was quickly released.[95]

More generally, this suggests that there are limits to what Tuareg integration can achieve in terms of preventing a resurgence of rebellion. The International Crisis Group notes, for instance, that the Tuareg mayor of Tchirozérine, Maha, joined the MNJ in 2007.[96] Grégoire also warns that it is not clear what degree of influence these former rebel leaders have on the younger generation of Tuareg, particularly those who came back from Libya.[97]

Meanwhile, AQIM-related attacks on Nigerien territory have not receded. To a large extent, these attacks have often been connected to Mali, with Nigerien criminal groups kidnapping Westerners to sell them to AQIM, who would then transfer them to Malian terri-

---

[92] Guichaoua, 2009, p. 11

[93] Guichaoua, 2009, p. 12.

[94] Sahel expert C, 2014.

[95] Ibrahim Diallo, "Insécurité: Abta Hamidine s'apprêtait à livrer les quatre otages français au clan Kadhafi," *Air info*, No. 122, June 15–30, 2011; Ibrahim Diallo "Niger: Aghali Alambo et Abta Hamidine, inculpés d'actes terroristes, libérés," *Afrik.com*, April 2, 2012; "Niger Arrests Ex–Rebel Chief on Suspected Qaeda Link," *Reuters*, March 21, 2012.

[96] International Crisis Group, 2013, p. 31, note 178.

[97] Grégoire, 2013, p. 10.

tory.[98] Table 5.2 shows that Westerners and Western interests—rather than the Nigerien military or civilian power—are the main targets of terrorist attacks in Niger. Although there have been several attacks against the Nigerien military since 2010—near Tilia in January 2010 and against the Tiloa military barracks in March 2010—AQIM did not claim responsibility for them, and their circumstances remain obscure.[99] One important exception, however, is the May 2013 attack against a Nigerien military base in Agadez. Overall, terrorist activity in Niger has resulted in a severe hit for the tourism industry, which was one of the main sources of revenue for local communities in the north and had already been hit hard by the 2007 rebellion.[100]

Although these old sources of instability still exist, some new ones have recently emerged as well. Compounding the threat of terrorist attacks, Boko Haram has shown an increased presence in Niger, which shares a border with Nigeria, over the past few years. The Nigerian group has been developing rear bases in the Diffa and Zinder regions in southern Niger, particularly since 2009 and the escalating military repression against the group by the Nigerian state.[101] Boko Haram also acts as an indirect source of instability because its violent attacks on civilians in Nigeria have resulted in population displacements toward Niger.[102] In addition, Nigeria expelled some Nigerien Boko Haram fighters back to their country of origin.[103] In June 2013, the escape of several high-profile terror suspects from Niamey's prison was attributed to the group.[104] In February 2014, Nigerien authorities arrested

[98] International Crisis Group, 2013, p. 40.

[99] International Crisis Group, 2013, p. 40, note 227.

[100] Sahel expert D, 2014; Alex Thurston, "Niger Braces for Regional Turbulence," *World Politics Review*, February 15, 2012a.

[101] International Crisis Group, 2013, p. 44; Grégoire, 2013, p. 11.

[102] International Crisis Group, 2013, p. 45.

[103] International Crisis Group, 2013, p. 45, note 259

[104] Sahel expert D, 2014; "Niger: L'attaque dans la prison de Niamey a été menée par des islamistes de Boko Haram," *Radio France internationale*, June 1, 2013.

Table 5.2
Attacks in Niger Related to al Qaeda in the Islamic Maghreb

Date	Location	Event	Outcome
December 2008	About 40 km from Niamey	Kidnapping of two Canadian diplomats	Hostages were released in April 2009
January 2009	Tassara department near Mali	Kidnapping of four Europeans	Three hostages were released in April and July 2009, one (Edwin Dyer) was killed
November 2009	Tahoua	Failed attempt to kidnap U.S. embassy staff members	No hostage taken
April 2010	Northern Niger	Kidnapping of a French engineer	Killed by AQIM in July 2010
September 2010	Arlit	Kidnapping of seven AREVA employees	Reportedly transferred to AQIM in Mali; three released in 2011; four released in October 2013
January 2011	Niamey	Kidnapping of two French people	Hostages killed during same-day rescue attempt
October 2012	Dakoro department	Kidnapping of six humanitarian workers	Five released in November 2012; one killed
May 2013	Arlit and Agadez	Coordinated attacks against a uranium mine and a military base	20 killed, dozens wounded

SOURCES: International Crisis Group, 2013, pp. 39–40; Steven Erlanger, "2 French Hostages Are Found Dead in Niger," *New York Times*, January 8, 2011; Abdoulaye Massalatchi, "Kidnapped Aid Workers Released in Niger, One Killed," *Reuters*, November 3, 2012; Abdoulaye Massalatchi, "Islamists Kill 20 in Suicide Attacks in Niger," *Reuters*, May 23, 2013; Mahamadou Issoufou, "Quatrième attaque terroriste au Niger, qui s'enfonce dans une nouvelle forme de guerre," *Radio France internationale*, June 13, 2013.

NOTE: This table does not include all reported terrorist attacks but only the ones that have been confirmed and have an established AQIM component. Some additional attacks might be due to criminal groups or Boko Haram.

20 Boko Haram militants suspected of planning attacks in the south of the country.[105]

In addition to this threat at its southern border, Niger has to face more difficulties on its eastern and western flanks. In the east, Niger is close to southwest Libya, which is ruled by militias and remains a trafficking hub. Libya might also be now home to some Jihadist groups that Operation Serval pushed out of Mali. According to the Nigerien government, the Agadez and Arlit bombings were prepared in Libya.[106] Grégoire describes the Ubari Valley in southern Libya as a "new safe haven" for Islamists.[107] Another consequence of the fall of Qadhafi that needs to be taken into account is the disappearance of Libyan mediation in the region's conflicts. To be certain, Libya was as much a source of instability as a source of stability; one reason Tandja was so opposed to negotiations with the MNJ in 2007 to 2009 was that he saw the group as a tool of Qadhafi to gain control of Niger's uranium and oil.[108] Still, during that rebellion, Libya led discussions between the warring parties and funded the disarmament of combatants.[109] It is unclear, as Libya went from being a source of diplomacy to being a nest of instability, what countries in the region could have enough influence and funds to play this type of mediating role.[110]

In the west, Mali remains an important source of instability. Retreating Islamists could use Niger as a rear base rather than go all the way to Libya.[111] If cross-border recruitment has been low for Tuareg rebel groups, things have been different for MUJWA, for which Niger

---

[105] Abdoulaye Massalaki, "Niger Arrests 20 Boko Haram Militants in Suspected Plot," *Reuters*, February 17, 2014.

[106] International Crisis Group, 2013, p. 38.

[107] Grégoire, 2013 p. 11.

[108] Raffray, 2013, p. 67.

[109] Grégoire, 2013, pp. 14, 37.

[110] Morocco and Algeria are likely candidates, but their deep antagonism over the status of the western Sahara could make their interference in the region more of a source of instability than stability.

[111] David J. Francis, "The Regional Impact of the Armed Conflict and French Intervention in Mali," Oslo: Norwegian Peacebuilding Resource Centre, April 9, 2013, p. 11.

appears to have represented a sizable recruiting ground—possibly because of Niger's geographical proximity with the Gao region, which has been MUJWA's stronghold.[112] Estimates of Nigerien MUJWA recruits vary widely. According to the International Crisis Group, about 100 young Nigerien Fula joined MUJWA in 2012 but moved back into the Tillabéri region of Niger after Operation Serval started.[113] Another source estimates that up to 3,000 Nigerien Fula might have joined MUJWA when the group took over parts of northern Mali in 2012, with most of them returning to Niger after France launched Operation Serval.[114] Religious radicalization could explain part of the attractiveness of MUJWA for Nigerien Fula, but, as in Mali, local dynamics are at least as important as religion to understand recruitment into, and affiliation with, armed groups. According to Nigerien Minister of Interior Abdou Labo, cited in a *Jeune Afrique* article, MUJWA's anti-Tuareg stance might have been attractive to Fula who happened to be in conflict with a local Tuareg clan.[115] The financial motive might have played a role as well, with each recruit receiving an estimated €500 to €1,000 to join the group.[116] MUJWA also reportedly developed economic and religious relationships with several Arab groups from the Tassara region bordering Mali.[117]

Finally, the Nigerien government has to face internal threats beyond its coup-prone military. An important one is the fact that the ambitious development programs that have been launched created expectations that might not be fulfilled. The PDES and SDS have yet to show direct, positive results on the economy and the general well-being of the population.[118] Programs face major challenges, first of

---

[112] Lebovich, 2013; International Crisis Group, 2013, p. 43.

[113] International Crisis Group, 2013, p. 43, note 245.

[114] Carayol, 2013b.

[115] Carayol, 2013b.

[116] Carayol, 2013b.

[117] Grégoire, 2013, p. 11.

[118] International Crisis Group, 2013, p. 20.

which are high unemployment levels and a sharp decline in the tourism industry due to security concerns.[119]

Meanwhile, these programs are costly. The Nigerien defense budget almost quadrupled between 2010 and 2014 (see Figure 5.2) to pay for higher salaries for military personnel, equipment, and recruitment.[120] These increases came at the expense of other categories of public spending: Niger reallocated close to $80 million from health and education to defense.[121] Emphasizing defense spending at the expense of other priorities could prove, in the longer term, a risky strategy. The population in Niamey suffers from power cuts despite promises that oil production and a new refinery would alleviate them, and much of the infrastructure in the entire country is in dire need of an upgrade or repairs.[122] Furthermore, there is a risk to cutting resources for funding such items as education in a country where 49.2 percent of the population in 2011 was under 15 and literacy rates are abysmal.[123] In April 2013, Niger experienced social unrest from unemployed youth in Diffa, as well as violent student demonstrations in Niamey in May 2014 due to delays in payments of scholarships on the part of the government.[124]

Finally, there is a possibility that Niger's participation in MINUSMA and the presence of U.S. and French troops could increase radicalization.[125] The International Crisis Group reports the existence of discontent in the army.[126] In February 2013, the United States deployed about 100 military personnel to Niger to manage a new pres-

---

[119] International Crisis Group, 2013, p. 33.

[120] Carayol, 2013b; Touchard, 2014.

[121] Tinti, 2013.

[122] Sahel expert D, 2014; Lebovich, 2013.

[123] Nigerien Ministry of Finance, *Le Niger en chiffres 2011*, November 2011, p. 30. In 2014, the literacy rate was 28.7 percent of people age 15 and above, according to UNDP's Human Development Indicators 2014 (UNDP, 2014).

[124] Moussa Kaka, "Niger: Manifestation des jeunes sans emploi de Diffa," *Radio France internationale*, April 30, 2013; "Niger: Au moins dix blessés, d'importants dégâts lors de violentes manifestations d'étudiants," *Pan Africa Press*, May 22, 2014.

[125] International Crisis Group, 2013, p. 42.

[126] International Crisis Group, 2013, p. 23.

Figure 5.2
Niger's Estimated Defense Budget, 2010–2014

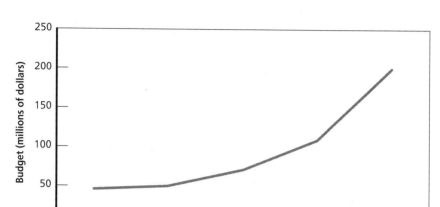

SOURCE: Touchard, 2014.
RAND *RR892-5.2*

ence for Predator drones flying out of Niamey on surveillance missions.[127] France has been granted access to the Niamey and Agadez
airports since 2013 and has been flying three Harfang surveillance
drones, as well as transport aircraft, in support to Operation Serval out
of them.[128] That same year, France added two U.S.-purchased Reaper
drones to its Niger-based fleet,[129] and the French air force base in Niger,
which has increased in size, can now accommodate Rafale aircraft, as
well as military aerial refueling aircraft (KC-135).[130] The shifting of
the French posture toward the Sahel announced by French Defense
Minister Jean-Yves Le Drian in January 2014 will make Niamey even
more critical to the French, who plan on making it their "Intelligence

---

[127] Craig Whitlock, "Drone Base in Niger Gives U.S. a Strategic Foothold in West Africa,"
Washington Post, March 21, 2013.

[128] International Crisis Group, 2013, p. 46; Fourt, 2013.

[129] "Lune de miel franco-américaine au Sahel," *Jeune Afrique*, March 10, 2014.

[130] Jean-Michel Bezat, "Uranium: pourquoi Areva peine à renouveler ses contrats au Niger,"
Le monde, March 25, 2014.

Division" in the Sahel.[131] As of early 2014, about 300 French military personnel were deployed in Niger undertaking missions in different domains: intelligence, counterterrorism, training of Nigerien forces, and interventions in the broader Sahel area.[132] Although Issoufou publicly welcomed both the French and U.S. presences and even volunteered to have Niger host the 2014 round of the U.S. flagship Flintlock military exercise in the Sahel, it remains to be seen whether the population shares this openness.[133]

Implications for Mali

Overall, it appears that some of Niger's structural characteristics make it more inherently stable than Mali. Its geographically mixed population, better-integrated Tuareg, and lesser north–south divide (mainly due to the fact that the north has some revenue that, unlike Mali, does not depend exclusively on tourism) provide some resilience in times of crisis. Issoufou's swift policy of securing borders and attempting to economically reintegrate returnees might have kept the worst at bay for Niger when Libya collapsed. However, the fact that our first two hypotheses might be true does not automatically disprove the third one. In other words, Niger might be more stable than Mali; its crisis-response strategy could be superior; and still, without luck, Niger might have experienced political unrest or a major security threat in spite of these because of all other existing factors of instability.

The case of Niger nonetheless suggests good practices that might not make a country impervious to instability but could at least increase its resistance to regional contagion. Some of these elements can hardly be replicated in Mali. One example is Niger's more-heterogeneous

---

[131] "Discours de Monsieur Jean-Yves le Drian ministre de la Défense devant le CSIS à Washington le vendredi 24 janvier 2014," French Ministry of Defense, January 24, 2014; "Map: France Revamps Military Operations in Africa's Sahel," *France 24*, updated May 9, 2014.

[132] Touchard, 2014; Véronique Barral, "Infographie: Les forces militaires françaises en Afrique," *Radio France internationale*, February 17, 2014.

[133] Issoufou cited in Whitlock, 2013; Tinti, Peter, "War, Peace and Civil Affairs in Niger," *Wall Street Journal*, March 6, 2014.

ethnic makeup. However, Mali could emulate some other elements of resilience. These include promoting the integration of minority communities, particularly Tuareg; lessening the north–south divide by improving basic services, as well as transportation infrastructure, to promote economic development and encourage geographic mobility; and fostering development to support decentralization and, in the long term, reduce risks of radicalization.

CHAPTER SIX

Conclusion

On balance, the accomplishments of the past peace accords in Mali have been thin. It would be an overstatement to conclude, however, that nothing has been achieved and that, in 2014, the situation stands as it did in 1990. Perhaps the biggest change since then is awareness: Northern interests, northern needs, and northern perspectives used to be unknown or ignored by the Malian government and the international community alike. Southerners, including some government officials, now devote more attention to northern matters. Second, an agreed-upon list of concerns (e.g., some autonomy and decentralization) now forms the framework for current and future talks. Third, the National Pact has irrevocably transformed the Malian political system. Democracy and decentralization, notwithstanding real failings and weaknesses, are permanent features of Malian political life. There was little doubt that the post-coup junta would eventually give way to an elected government. It is also worth reiterating a fact that is not immediately obvious given all the recent violence: Most northerners did not participate in the fighting and have a vested interest in stability.

As for the implementation of past accords, it is indisputable that nothing has been implemented as effectively as one might have wished, regardless of whether any of the problems can be attributed to bad faith on the part of Bamako. It remains true nonetheless that two elements of the accords that have been implemented at least in part receive positive reviews notwithstanding their problems: the integration of northern fighters into the Malian army and decentralization and democratization. Both programs appear valuable so far.

What has been missing so far is a lack of representation, a problem that stems in part from mistaken assumptions about the representativeness of the rebel groups that have been parties to past peace accords, as well as from efforts to include northerners and legitimate northern voices, such as the traditional chiefs, that have been, in some northern eyes, inadequate. This relates to the question of security, the inability of Mali's security forces to provide it, the inappropriateness of deploying them in their current form to try, and the consequent need to somehow enlist the support of northern communities. One question that needs to be asked is how the rebel-integration program can be expanded or adapted such that northerners no longer regard Mali's army as a foreign military, and vice versa. Indeed, the *republican* character of Mali's army could be at least as important as its ability to fight, something that U.S. security assistance should keep in mind. Another question that needs to be asked is how Mali's current form of democracy and its administrative system can be strengthened, supplemented, or otherwise adapted to foster the state's legitimacy and enhance identification with it. The call for giving a specific role to traditional chiefs on board so as to prevent them from undermining democracy is intriguing and merits further consideration.

Similarly, the chiefs and other community leaders could well hold the key for security assistance. The French colonial model of relying on one or a few militias would no longer work because of the political implications of elevating certain fractions above others. However, there are other models for organizing local forces that are less fraught.

Niger, too, offers important lessons with respect to alternative government policy approaches to integrating Tuareg into government and the value of development. After all, the lack of basic services in the north of Mali remains an issue. Islamist groups that took over the northern cities in 2012 were aware of this and used it as an opportunity to gain the population's support (provision of a hotline number that people could call if they were being robbed or harassed;[1] cleaning of gutters that had not been cleaned in years). AQIM leaders were

---

[1]   Morten Bøås and Liv Elin Torheim, "Mali Unmasked: Resistance, Collusion, Collaboration," Oslo: Norwegian Peacebuilding Resource Centre, March 15, 2013, p. 3.

particularly aware of the importance of cultivating popular support, as evidenced by the group's internal documents found in Timbuktu after Operation Serval began.[2] Niger is hardly a model—how politically stable it really is remains to be seen in the longer term—but its resilience in the face of the Malian crisis suggests that the policies adopted by Issoufou coupling security and development programs could have been beneficial. Niger might have also benefited from its less drastic north–south divide, which Mali can emulate through better communication infrastructure and public services in the north. Finally, Niger's more-successful integration of Tuareg into its state structures is both a result of its more-mixed population and voluntarist policies. Mali can emulate the latter, which will also help remind its minorities that they represent an integral part of the Malian nation.

Finally, it should also be clear that no silver bullet will fix Mali's problems, certainly not overnight. Mali's jihadist problem is nested within a larger security problem, which is, in turn, nested within several other problems, ranging from economics to governance. The same combination of security and development measures that have been tried in Niger and, with equally mixed success, in Mali since 1992 remain the key to future stability. In Mali, however, implementing them in a way that is both sufficiently effective to make a difference on the ground and not so drastic as so antagonize southern populations will be a most delicate balance to strike.

---

[2]   Rukmini Callimachi, "In Timbuktu, al-Qaida Left Behind a Manifesto," *Big Story*, February 14, 2013.

References

"5 Year Uranium Prices and Price Chart," *InvestmentMine*, undated; referenced June 2014. As of November 11, 2014:
http://www.infomine.com/investment/metal-prices/uranium-oxide/5-year/

Abdoulaye, Ibbo, "10 Arrested in Niger Coup Attempt, President Says," *CNN*, August 3, 2011. As of November 10, 2014:
http://www.cnn.com/2011/WORLD/africa/08/03/niger.coup.arrest/

Accord préliminaire à l'élection présidentielle et aux pourparlers inclusifs de paix au Mali [Preliminary agreement for the presidential election and inclusive peace talks in Mali], Ouagadougou, Burkina Faso, June 18, 2013. As of November 10, 2014:
http://peacemaker.un.org/mali-accord-preliminaire-elections2013

Accord sur la cessation des hostilités: Le gouvernement de la République du Mali d'une part et le Mouvement Populaire de l'Azaouad et le Front Islamique Arabe d'autre part [Agreement on the cessation of hostilities: The government of the Republic of Mali on the one hand and the Popular Movement Azaouad and the Arab Islamic Front on the other], Tamanrasset, Algeria, January 6, 1991. As of November 10, 2014:
http://www.unesco.org/culture/fr/indigenous/Dvd/pj/TOUAREG/TouaregC4_2.pdf

Accords d'Alger de 2006: Restauration de la paix, de la sécurité et du développement dans la région de Kidal [Algiers Accords of 2006: Restoration of peace, security, and development in the region of Kidal], July 4, 2006. As of November 10, 2014:
http://peacemaker.un.org/sites/peacemaker.un.org/files/ML_060704_Accord%20d%27Alger.pdf

"Accord stratégique entre le Niger et Areva sur les mines d'uranium," *Liberation*, May 26, 2014.

Algiers Accords—*See* Accords d'Alger de 2006, 2006.

Arab leader A, interview with Michael Shurkin, Bamako, October 11, 2013.

Arab leader B, interview with Michael Shurkin, Bamako, October 8, 2013.

Armstrong, Hannah, "Crisis in Mali: Root Causes and Long-Term Solutions," Washington, D.C.: United States Institute of Peace, Brief 149, May 31, 2013. As of November 10, 2014:
http://www.usip.org/publications/
crisis-in-mali-root-causes-and-long-term-solutions

"ATT à la cloture du forum de Kidal," *Maliweb*, March 27, 2007. As of November 10, 2014:
http://www.maliweb.net/category.php?NID=17184

"Au Niger, le président Issoufou dénonce une tentative de coup d'État," *Radio France internationale*, August 3, 2011. As of November 11, 2014:
http://www.rfi.fr/afrique/
20110803-niger-le-president-issoufou-denonce-tentative-coup-etat/

Auty, Richard M., *Sustaining Development in Mineral Economies: The Resource Curse Thesis*, London: Routledge, 1993.

Barral, Véronique, "Infographie: Les forces militaires françaises en Afrique," *Radio France internationale*, February 17, 2014. As of November 10, 2014:
http://www.rfi.fr/afrique/
20140217-infographie-mouvements-forces-militaires-francaises-afrique/

Bellah leader, interview with Michael Shurkin, Bamako, October 8, 2013.

Benchérif, Adib, "Résilience d'Al-Qaïda au Maghreb islamique au nord du Mali," *Réflexion*, November 12, 2013.

Berabiche leader, interview with Michael Shurkin, Bamako, October 4, 2013.

Berghezan, Georges, *Panorama du trafic de cocaïne en Afrique de l'ouest*, Brussels: Groupe de Recherche et d'Information sur la Paix et la Sécurité, June 1, 2012. As of November 10, 2014:
http://www.grip.org/en/node/39

Bezat, Jean-Michel, "Uranium: pourquoi Areva peine à renouveler ses contrats au Niger," *Le monde*, March 25, 2014. As of November 10, 2014:
http://www.lemonde.fr/economie/article/2014/03/25/
uranium-pourquoi-areva-peine-a-renouveler-ses-contrats-au-niger_4389487_3234.
html

Biamoye, Hamma, "'Nous pas bouger,' le mouvement de résistance de la jeunesse de Gao qui a fait le choix des islamistes," *Les observateurs*, July 9, 2012. As of November 11, 2014:
http://observers.france24.com/fr/content/20120709-mali-gao-nord-manifestation-
jeunes-mnla-mujao-nous-pas-bouger-resistance-islamistes-patrouilleurs

Bøås, Morten, and Liv Elin Torheim, "Mali Unmasked: Resistance, Collusion, Collaboration," Oslo: Norwegian Peacebuilding Resource Centre, March 15, 2013. As of November 10, 2014:
http://www.peacebuilding.no/Regions/Africa/Mali/Publications/
Mali-unmasked-resistance-collusion-collaboration

Boilley, Pierre, *Les Touaregs Kel Adagh: Dépendances et révoltes—du Soudan français au Mali contemporain*, Paris: Éd. Karthala, 1999.

Boisbouvier, Christophe, "Uranium: le Niger n'a 'rien à cacher' sur l'accord avec Areva," *Radio France internationale*, June 4, 2014. As of November 10, 2014:
http://www.rfi.fr/afrique/20140604-uranium-le-niger-rien-cacher-accord-areva/

Boukhari, Sophie, "Mali: A Flickering Flame," *UNESCO Courier*, Vol. 53, No. 1, January 2000, pp. 26–28. As of November 10, 2014:
http://unesdoc.unesco.org/Ulis/cgi-bin/
ulis.pl?catno=118499&set=4F4CFF3F_0_239&gp=&lin=1&ll=c

Bozonnet, Charlotte, "Niger Remains Wary of Mali Crisis on Its Doorstep," *Guardian*, March 5, 2013. As of November 10, 2014:
http://www.theguardian.com/world/2013/mar/05/niger-conflict-mali-army

Callimachi, Rukmini, "In Timbuktu, al-Qaida Left Behind a Manifesto," *Big Story*, February 14, 2013. As of November 10, 2014:
http://bigstory.ap.org/article/timbuktu-al-qaida-left-behind-strategic-plans

Carayol, Rémi, "Mali: Le martyre de Gao," *Jeune Afrique*, February 25, 2013a. As of November 10, 2014:
http://www.jeuneafrique.com/Article/JA2719p032_036_01.xml0/

———, "Niger, au milieu du chaos," *Jeune Afrique*, April 24, 2013b. As of November 10, 2014:
http://www.jeuneafrique.com/Article/JA2727p028.xml0/

———, "Niger: Le pays où les Touaregs bénéficient de la décentralisation," *Jeune Afrique*, May 22, 2013c. As of November 10, 2014:
http://www.jeuneafrique.com/Article/JA2731p037.xml0/

Central Intelligence Agency, "Mali," last updated June 20, 2014a. As of November 17, 2014:
https://www.cia.gov/library/publications/the-world-factbook/geos/ml.html

———, "Niger," last updated June 20, 2014b. As of November 17, 2014:
https://www.cia.gov/library/publications/the-world-factbook/geos/ng.html

Chivvis, Christopher S., and Andrew Liepman, *North Africa's Menace: AQIM's Evolution and the U.S. Policy Response*, Santa Monica, Calif.: RAND Corporation, RR-415-OSD, 2013. As of November 10, 2014:
http://www.rand.org/pubs/research_reports/RR415.html

Claudot-Hawad, Hélène, "La fragmentation touarègue ou le prix de la 'paix,'" in Hélène Claudot-Hawad, ed., *Touaregs: Voix solitaires sous l'horizon confisqué*, Paris: Ethnies/Survival International, 1996, pp. 37–53.

Coulibaly, Be, "États généraux de la décentralisation: Des recommandations pour mieux faire," *L'essor*, November 1, 2013.

"Des opposants arrêtés et un journal fermé au Niger," *Le monde*, May 25, 2014. As of November 10, 2014:
http://www.lemonde.fr/afrique/article/2014/05/25/des-opposants-arretes-et-un-journal-ferme-au-niger_4425335_3212.html

Deycard, Frédéric, *Les rébellions touarègues du Niger: Combattants, mobilisation et culture politique*, Institut d'études politiques de Bordeaux, doctoral thesis, January 12, 2011.

Diakité, Madiassa Kaba, "Les jeunes de Gao se désolent du manque de reconnaissance de l'état," *Le républicain*, April 15, 2013.

Diallo, Ibrahim, "Insécurité: Abta Hamidine s'apprêtait à livrer les quatre otages français au clan Kadhafi," *Aïr info*, No. 122, June 15–30, 2011. As of November 11, 2014:
http://nigerdiaspora.info/journaux/AirInfo_15_06_11.pdf

———, "Niger: Aghali Alambo et Abta Hamidine, inculpés d'actes terroristes, libérés," *Afrik.com*, April 2, 2012. As of November 10, 2014:
http://www.afrik.com/article25219.html

"Discours de Monsieur Jean-Yves le Drian ministre de la Défense devant le CSIS à Washington le vendredi 24 janvier 2014," French Ministry of Defense, January 24, 2014. As of November 11, 2014:
http://www.defense.gouv.fr/ministre/prises-de-parole-du-ministre/prises-de-parole-de-m.-jean-yves-le-drian/discours-de-monsieur-jean-yves-le-drian-ministre-de-la-defense-devant-le-csis-a-washington-le-vendredi-24-janvier-2014

Djire, D., "Situation à Kidal: Les vérités du député Ahmoudène AG Iknass," *L'essor*, December 27, 2013.

Erlanger, Steven, "2 French Hostages Are Found Dead in Niger," *New York Times*, January 8, 2011. As of November 11, 2014:
http://www.nytimes.com/2011/01/09/world/africa/09niger.html

———, "France Is Increasing Security at Sites in Niger and at Home," *New York Times*, January 24, 2013. As of November 11, 2014:
http://www.nytimes.com/2013/01/25/world/europe/france-is-increasing-security-at-uranium-sites-in-niger.html

Filiu, Jean-Pierre, *Could Al-Qaeda Turn African in the Sahel?* Washington, D.C.: Carnegie Endowment for International Peace, June 10, 2010. As of November 11, 2014:
http://carnegieendowment.org/2010/06/10/could-al-qaeda-turn-african-in-sahel

Florquin, Nicolas, and Stephanie Pezard, "Insurgency, Disarmament, and Insecurity in Northern Mali, 1990–2004," in Nicolas Florquin and Eric G. Berman, eds., *Armed and Aimless: Armed Groups, Guns, and Human Security in the ECOWAS Region*, Geneva: Small Arms Survey, May 2005, pp. 46–77. As of November 11, 2014:
http://www.smallarmssurvey.org/publications/by-type/book-series/armed-and-aimless.html

Fourt, Olivier, "Le Niger, un 'point d'appui' opérationnel pour la France," *Radio France internationale*, last modified May 28, 2013. As of November 11, 2014:
http://www.rfi.fr/afrique/20130527-le-niger-point-appui-operationnel-france/

Francis, David J., "The Regional Impact of the Armed Conflict and French Intervention in Mali," Oslo: Norwegian Peacebuilding Resource Centre, April 9, 2013. As of November 11, 2014:
http://www.peacebuilding.no/Regions/Africa/Mali/Publications/The-regional-impact-of-the-armed-conflict-and-French-intervention-in-Mali

Giroux, Greg, "Voters Throw Bums in While Holding Congress in Disdain," *Bloomberg*, December 13, 2012. As of November 11, 2014:
http://www.bloomberg.com/news/2012-12-13/voters-throw-bums-in-while-disdaining-congress-bgov-barometer.html

Grégoire, Emmanuel, *Touaregs du Niger, le destin d'un mythe*, new ed., Paris: Karthala, 2010.

———, "Islamistes et rebelles touaregs maliens: Alliances, rivalités et ruptures," *Sur le vif*, July 3, 2013.

Grémont, Charles, *Les Touaregs Iwellemedan (1647–1896): Un ensemble politique de la Boucle du Niger*, Paris: Karthala, 2010a.

———, *Touaregs et Arabes dans les forces armées coloniales et maliennes: Une histoire en trompe-l'œil*, Paris: Institut français des relations internationales, 2010b. As of November 11, 2014:
http://ifri.org/?page=detail-contribution&id=6118&idprovenance=97

Guede, Boubacar, "Niger: Le président Issoufou lance un appel aux rebelles maliens," *Radio France internationale*, February 14, 2012.

Guichaoua, Yvan, *Circumstantial Alliances and Loose Loyalties in Rebellion Making: The Case of Tuareg Insurgency in Northern Niger (2007–2009)*, A Micro Level Analysis of Violent Conflict Research Working Paper 20, December 2009. As of November 11, 2014:
http://www.microconflict.eu/publications/RWP20_YG.pdf

Guindo, Amadou Salif, "Mme Assory Aicha Belco Maiga, présidente du conseil de cercle de Tessalit à propos de la libération de Gao 'Ma joie ne sera totale que quand Tombouctou et Kidal seront reprises,'" *La Dépêche*, January 30, 2013.

Gutelius, David, "Islam in Northern Mali and the War on Terror," *Journal of Contemporary African Studies*, Vol. 25, No. 1, 2007, pp. 59–76.

Haddad, Aïda, "Maroc-Mali: Renforcement du partenariat dans les mines et les hydrocarbures," *Le point*, May 14, 2014. As of November 11, 2014:
http://www.lepoint.fr/afrique/economie/maroc-mali-renforcement-du-partenariat-dans-les-mines-et-les-hydrocarbures-14-05-2014-1822797_2033.php

HCME Allemagne, "Jeunes patriotes de Gao," *YouTube*, November 25, 2012. As of November 11, 2014:
http://www.youtube.com/watch?v=fs1j-w-ufd4

Human Rights Watch, "Niger: Warring Sides Must End Abuses of Civilians," December 20, 2007. As of November 11, 2014:
http://www.hrw.org/news/2007/12/19/
niger-warring-sides-must-end-abuses-civilians

———, "Mali: Ensure Justice for Grave Abuses," March 21, 2014. As of November 11, 2014:
http://www.hrw.org/news/2014/03/21/mali-ensure-justice-grave-abuses

Integrated Regional Information Networks, "Mali: Indignation Dominates Reaction as Attacks in North Escalate," August 31, 2007. As of November 11, 2014:
http://www.irinnews.org/report/74058/
mali-indignation-dominates-reaction-as-attacks-in-north-escalate

International Crisis Group, *Mali: Éviter l'escalade*, Brussels, Africa Report 189, July 18, 2012. As of November 11, 2014:
http://www.crisisgroup.org/~/media/files/africa/west-africa/mali/
189-mali-eviter-l-escalade.pdf

———, *Niger: Another Weak Link in the Sahel?* Brussels, Africa Report 208, September 19, 2013. As of November 11, 2014:
http://www.crisisgroup.org/en/regions/africa/west-africa/niger/
208-niger-another-weak-link-in-the-sahel.aspx

———, *Mali: Reform or Relapse*, Brussels, Africa Report 210, January 10, 2014. As of November 11, 2014:
http://www.crisisgroup.org/en/regions/africa/west-africa/mali/
210-mali-reform-or-relapse.aspx

"Interview de Ibrahim Bahanga: 'L'alliance entre le MNJ et nous existe depuis que nous avons reçu des formations militaires en Libye,'" *L'indépendant* (Bamako), August 30, 2007.

Issoufou, Mahamadou, "Quatrième attaque terroriste au Niger, qui s'enfonce dans une nouvelle forme de guerre," *Radio France internationale*, June 13, 2013. As of November 11, 2014:
http://www.rfi.fr/afrique/
20130612-quatrieme-attaque-terroriste-niger-menace-une-nouvelle-forme-guerre/

Kaka, Moussa, "Niger: Manifestation des jeunes sans emploi de Diffa," *Radio France internationale*, April 30, 2013. As of November 11, 2014:
http://www.rfi.fr/emission/20130430-niger-manifestations-jeunes-emploi-diffa/

Kappès-Grangé, Anne, "Niger: Le Premier ministre Brigi Rafini, en toute discrétion," *Jeune Afrique*, November 7, 2011. As of November 11, 2014:
http://www.jeuneafrique.com/Article/ARTJAJA2651p046.xml0/

Keita, Modibo, *La résolution du conflit touareg au Mali et au Niger*, Groupe de recherche sur les interventions de paix dans les conflits intra-étatiques, Note de recherche 10, July 2002.

Koné, Assane, "Résolution de la crise malienne: Recommandations des états généraux de la décentralisation," *Notre nation*, October 28, 2013. As of November 11, 2014:
http://notrenation.com/?Resolution-de-la-crise-malienne

Lamine, Mohamed, "Gao: La population en meeting de protestation contre le gouvernement de transition," *Ouest Afrika Blog*, June 5, 2013. As of November 11, 2014:
http://ouestafrikablog.net/blog/2013/06/05/gao-la-population-en-meeting-de-protestation-contre-le-gouvernement-de-transition/

"Lancement au Niger d'une stratégie de développement et de sécurité," *Panapress*, October 2, 2012. As of November 11, 2014:
http://www.panapress.com/Lancement-au-Niger-d-une-strategie-de-developpement-et-de-securite--13-845310-0-lang4-index.html

Lazuta, Jennifer, "Niger Signs Long-Delayed Uranium Deal with Areva," *Voice of America*, May 27, 2014. As of November 11, 2014:
http://www.voanews.com/content/
niger-signs-long-delayed-uranium-deal-with-areva/1923567.html

Lea, David, and Annamarie Rowe, eds., *A Political Chronology of Africa*, London: Europa Publications, 2001.

Le Billon, Véronique, "Uranium: Areva et le Niger scellent un nouvel accord," *Les échos*, May 26, 2014. As of November 11, 2014:
http://www.lesechos.fr/economie-france/conjoncture/
0203524926656-uranium-areva-et-le-niger-scellent-un-nouvel-accord-673782.php

Lebovich, Andrew, "Overstating Terror in Niger: Letter from Niamey," *Foreign Affairs*, August 14, 2013. As of November 11, 2014:
http://www.foreignaffairs.com/features/letters-from/overstating-terror-in-niger

Lecocq, Jean Sebastian, *That Desert Is Our Country: Tuareg Rebellions and Competing Nationalisms in Contemporary Mali (1946–1996)*, Amsterdam: Universiteit von Amsterdam, doctoral thesis, 2002.

———, *Disputed Desert: Decolonisation, Competing Nationalism and Tuareg Rebellions in Northern Mali*, Leiden: Brill, 2010.

Le Hir, Pierre, "Réduire à 50% la part du nucléaire en France, crédible ou non?" *Le monde*, December 5, 2013. As of November 11, 2014:
http://www.lemonde.fr/planete/article/2013/12/04/
reduire-a-50-la-part-du-nucleaire-en-france-credible-ou-non_3525288_3244.html

"Le Niger s'enfonce dans une crise politique," *Jeune Afrique*, June 5, 2014. As of November 10, 2014:
http://www.jeuneafrique.com/actu/20140605T064324Z20140605T064310Z/

"L'honorable Assarid Ag Imbarcaouane sur l'ORTM: 'Les populations du nord n'accepteront jamais le retour du MNLA dans les villes,'" *L'indépendant*, February 11, 2013.

"Liste des nouveaux députés: Abeibara," *aBamako.com*, undated. As of December 3, 2014:
http://www.abamako.com/elections/legislatives/2013/election/
Cercle.asp?R=8&C=47&P=#gsc.tab=0

"Liste des nouveaux députés: Kidal" *aBamako.com*, undated. As of December 3, 2014:
http://www.abamako.com/elections/legislatives/2013/election/
Cercle.asp?R=8&C=46&P=#gsc.tab=0

"Liste des nouveaux députés: Mali," *aBamako.com*, undated. As of December 3, 2014:
http://www.abamako.com/ELECTIONS/legislatives/2013/#gsc.tab=0

"Liste des nouveaux députés: Tessalit," *aBamako.com*, undated. As of December 3, 2014:
http://www.abamako.com/elections/legislatives/2013/election/
Cercle.asp?R=8&C=48&P=#gsc.tab=0

"Liste des nouveaux députés: Tin-Essako," *aBamako.com*, undated. As of December 3, 2014:
http://www.abamako.com/elections/legislatives/2013/election/
Cercle.asp?R=8&C=49&P=#gsc.tab=0

"Lune de miel franco-américaine au Sahel," *Jeune Afrique*, March 10, 2014. As of November 11, 2014:
http://www.jeuneafrique.com/Article/JA2773p008.xml5/

Lyammouri, Rida, "Understanding Who's Who in Northern Mali: Terrorists Secessionists and Criminals," panel presentation, Johns Hopkins University School of Advanced International Studies, Washington, D.C., March 11, 2013. As of November 11, 2014:
https://www.youtube.com/watch?v=nkJOiygOsP8

MAA commander—*See* Mouvement arabe de l'Azawad commander.

Malian journalist, phone interview with Stephanie Pezard, August 2009.

"Mali: Bilan positif pour les États généraux de la décentralisation," *Radio France internationale*, October 24, 2013. As of November 11, 2014:
http://www.rfi.fr/afrique/
20131024-mali-bilan-positif-fin-etats-generaux-decentralisation/

"Mali: Des membres d'Ansar Dine font sécession et créent leur propre mouvement," *Radio France internationale*, January 24, 2013. As of November 11, 2014:
http://www.rfi.fr/afrique/20130124-mali-membres-ansar-dine-font-secession-creent-leur-propre-mouvement-mouvement-islamique-azawad/

Mamane, Dalatou Malam, "Mission de l'Unité de Fusion et de Liaison (UFL) au Niger: La lutte contre le terrorisme plus que jamais engagée par les Forces de Défense et de Sécurité nigériennes," *Le Sahel*, No. 8306, April 3, 2012.

"Manifestation à Gao: Quand les revendications se font sociales," *Radio France internationale*, October 11, 2013. As of November 12, 2014:
http://www.rfi.fr/afrique/
20131011-mali-manifestants-gao-revendications-sociales-jeunes-femmes-insecurite/

"Map: France Revamps Military Operations in Africa's Sahel," *France 24*, updated May 9, 2014. As of November 11, 2014:
http://www.france24.com/en/
20140508-infographic-france-military-in-africa-sahel-le-drian-mali-chad/

Marchal, Roland, "The Coup in Mali: The Result of a Long-Term Crisis or Spillover from the Libyan Civil War?" Oslo: Norwegian Peacebuilding Resource Centre, May 2012. As of November 11, 2014:
http://www.peacebuilding.no/Regions/Africa/Mali/Publications/The-coup-in-Mali-the-result-of-a-long-term-crisis-or-spillover-from-the-Libyan-civil-war

Massalaki, Abdoulaye, "Niger Arrests 20 Boko Haram Militants in Suspected Plot," *Reuters*, February 17, 2014. As of November 18, 2014:
http://www.reuters.com/article/2014/02/17/
us-niger-bokoharam-plot-idUSBREA1G0TV20140217

Massalatchi, Abdoulaye, "Kidnapped Aid Workers Released in Niger, One Killed," *Reuters*, November 3, 2012. As of November 11, 2014:
http://www.reuters.com/article/2012/11/03/
us-niger-kidnapping-release-idUSBRE8A205E20121103

———, "Islamists Kill 20 in Suicide Attacks in Niger," *Reuters*, May 23, 2013. As of November 11, 2014:
http://www.reuters.com/article/2013/05/23/
us-niger-attacks-idUSBRE94M09N20130523

McGregor, Andrew, "Red Berets, Green Berets: Can Mali's Divided Military Restore Order and Stability?" *Terrorism Monitor*, Vol. 11, No. 4, February 22, 2013. As of November 11, 2014:
http://www.jamestown.org/single/
?tx_ttnews%5Btt_news%5D=40493&no_cache=1

"Mise en œuvre du PDES 2012–2015: Un instrument de référence pour impulser une mutation qualitative de l'économie nigérienne," *Le Sahel*, undated; referenced June 2014. As of November 11, 2014:
http://www.lesahel.org/index.php/economie/item/2830-mise-en-%C5%93uvre-du-pdes-2012-2015--un-instrument-de-r%C3%A9f%C3%A9rence-pour-impulser-une-mutation-qualitative-de-l%C3%A9conomie-nig%C3%A9rienne

MNA—*See* Mouvement National de l'Azawad.

Mouvement arabe de l'Azawad commander, interview with Michael Shurkin, Bamako, October 8, 2013.

Mouvement National de l'Azawad, "Le Mouvement national de l'Azawad condamne le PSPSDN," *Journal du Mali*, September 4, 2011. As of November 11, 2014:
http://www.journaldumali.com/article.php?aid=3590

Naik, Asmita, *Returnees from Libya: The Bittersweet Experience of Coming Home*, Geneva: International Organization for Migration, Policy in Brief, May 2012. As of November 11, 2014:
http://publications.iom.int/bookstore/free/Policy_In_Brief.pdf

National Pact—*See* Pacte national conclu entre le gouvernement de la République du Mali et les Mouvements et fronts unifiés de l'Azawad consacrant le statut particulier du Nord du Mali, 1992.

Niangaly, Abdoulaye, "Lancement officiel du PSPSDN: Enfin le bout du tunnel pour le Nord du Mali," *Le Prétoire* (Bamako), August 11, 2011.

Niezen, Ronald Wesley, *Diverse Styles of Islamic Reform Among the Songhay of Eastern Mali*, Cambridge, UK: Cambridge University, thesis, October 27, 1987. As of November 12, 2014:
https://www.repository.cam.ac.uk/handle/1810/227576

"Niger Arrests Ex–Rebel Chief on Suspected Qaeda Link," *Reuters*, March 21, 2012. As of November 12, 2014:
http://www.reuters.com/article/2012/03/21/
ozatp-niger-rebel-idAFJOE82K03N20120321

"Niger: Au moins dix blessés, d'importants dégâts lors de violentes manifestations d'étudiants," *Pan Africa Press*, May 22, 2014. As of November 10, 2014:
http://www.panafricapress.com/9035?lang=fr

Niger expert, conversation with Stephanie Pezard, June 2014.

"Niger: L'attaque dans la prison de Niamey a été menée par des islamistes de Boko Haram," *Radio France internationale*, June 1, 2013. As of November 11, 2014:
http://www.rfi.fr/afrique/
20130601-niger-prison-niamey-attaquee-groupe-arme-boko-haram/

"Niger Suicide Bombers Target Areva Mine and Barracks," *BBC*, May 23, 2013. As of November 11, 2014:
http://www.bbc.co.uk/news/world-africa-22637084

Nigerien Ministry of Finance, *Le Niger en chiffres 2011*, November 2011. As of November 11, 2014:
http://www.stat-niger.org/statistique/file/Annuaires_Statistiques/
Annuaire_ins_2011/Niger%20en%20chiffres%20nov%202011.pdf

Nigerien Prime Minister's Office, "Synthèse PAP SE/SDS Sahel-Niger," briefing, November 26, 2013. As of November 11, 2014:
http://www.sds-sahelniger.ne/index.php/plan-d-action

Ouagadougou Accord—*See* Accord préliminaire à l'élection présidentielle et aux pourparlers inclusifs de paix au Mali, 2013.

Pacte national conclu entre le gouvernement de la République du Mali et les Mouvements et fronts unifiés de l'Azawad consacrant le statut particulier du Nord du Mali [National Pact between the government of the Republic of Mali and the United Movements and Fronts of Azawad dedicating the special status of northern Mali], Bamako, April 11, 1992.

Pellerin, Mathieu, "La résilience nigérienne à l'épreuve de la guerre au Mali," *L'Afrique en questions*, No. 15, Institut français de relations internationales, February 2013. As of November 11, 2014:
http://www.ifri.org/?page=detail-contribution&id=7545

Pezard, Stephanie, and Michael Shurkin, *Toward a Secure and Stable Mali: Approaches to Engaging Local Actors*, Santa Monica, Calif.: RAND Corporation, RR-296-OSD, 2013. As of November 11, 2014:
http://www.rand.org/pubs/research_reports/RR296.html

Porter, Geoff D., "AQIM's Objectives in North Africa," *CTC Sentinel*, Vol. 4, No. 2, February 2011, pp. 5–8. As of November 11, 2014:
https://www.ctc.usma.edu/posts/aqim%E2%80%99s-objectives-in-north-africa

Raffray, Mériadec, "Les rébellions touarègues au Sahel," French Ministry of Defense, July 1, 2013. As of November 11, 2014:
http://www.cdef.terre.defense.gouv.fr/publications/cahier-du-retex/recherche/
les-rebellions-touaregues-au-sahel

Roberto, "El gobierno del Azawad," *A modo de esperanza*, June 20, 2012. As of November 12, 2014:
http://amododeesperanza.blogspot.com/2012/06/el-gobierno-del-azawad.html

Sachs, Jeffrey D., and Andrew M. Warner, "The Curse of Natural Resources," *European Economic Review*, Vol. 45, 2001, pp. 827–838.

Sahel expert A, phone interview with Michael Shurkin, December 11, 2012.

Sahel expert B, phone interview with Stephanie Pezard, April 22, 2014.

Sahel expert C, phone interview with Stephanie Pezard, April 24, 2014.

Sahel expert D, written correspondence with Stephanie Pezard, September 3, 2014.

Salifou, André, *La question touarègue au Niger*, Paris: Karthala, 1993.

Scheele, Judith, "Tribus, états et fraude: La région frontalière algéro-malienne," *Études rurales*, Vol. 184, February 2009, pp. 79–94.

Schnapper, Dominique, *La communauté des citoyens: Sur l'idée moderne de nation*, Paris: Gallimard, 1994.

Seely, Jennifer C., "A Political Analysis of Decentralisation: Coopting the Tuareg Threat in Mali," *Journal of Modern African Studies*, Vol. 39, No. 3, 2001, pp. 499–524.

Sidibé, Kalilou, *Security Management in Northern Mali: Criminal Networks and Conflict Resolution Mechanisms*, Brighton, UK: Institute of Development Studies, Research Report 77, August 2012. As of November 12, 2014: http://www.ids.ac.uk/publication/security-management-in-northern-mali-criminal-networks-and-conflict-resolution-mechanisms

Simpere, Anne-Sophie, and Ali Idrissa, *Niger: À qui profite l'uranium? L'enjeu de la renégociation des contrats miniers d'AREVA*, Oxfam, November 2013. As of November 11, 2014: http://www.oxfam.org/sites/www.oxfam.org/files/niger_renegociations_areva_note_oxfam-rotab.pdf

Songhai leader A, phone interview with Michael Shurkin, October 8, 2013.

Songhai leader B, phone interview with Michael Shurkin, February 11, 2014.

Stratfor, "Niger: A Rebel Threat to the Uranium Sector," Austin, Texas, February 1, 2008.

Takiou, Chahana, "Entretien avec Mohamed Ould Mataly, ancien député de Bourem: 'Je ne suis pas du MUJAO,'" *22 Septembre*, July 12, 2012. As of November 12, 2014: http://www.maliweb.net/politique/entretien-avec-mohamed-ould-mataly-ancien-depute-de-bourem-je-ne-suis-pas-du-mujao-79362.html

Tamanrasset Accord—*See* Accord sur la cessation des hostilités, 1991.

Thienot, Dorothée, "Mali: Des patrouilleurs pour remplacer l'Etat à Gao," *Slate Afrique*, January 17, 2013. As of November 12, 2014: http://www.slateafrique.com/101293/mali-gao-patrouilleurs-remplacent-etat-gao

Thiolay, Boris, "Mali: La guerre de la cocaïne," *L'express*, March 21, 2013. As of November 12, 2014:
http://www.lexpress.fr/actualite/monde/afrique/
mali-la-guerre-de-la-cocaine_1233028.html

Thurston, Alex, "Niger Braces for Regional Turbulence," *World Politics Review*, February 15, 2012a. As of November 12, 2014:
http://www.worldpoliticsreview.com/articles/11479/
niger-braces-for-regional-turbulence

———, "Niger Secures $4.8 Billion for Security and Development: Is This a Regional Model?" *Sahel Blog*, November 16, 2012b. As of November 12, 2014:
http://sahelblog.wordpress.com/2012/11/16/
niger-secures-4-8-billion-for-security-and-development-is-this-a-regional-model/

Tinti, Peter, "Niger: The Stable Sahelian State, for Now," *Think Africa Press*, September 27, 2013. As of November 12, 2014:
http://thinkafricapress.com/niger/stable-instability-sahelian-state-mali-example

———, "War, Peace and Civil Affairs in Niger," *Wall Street Journal*, March 6, 2014. As of November 12, 2014:
http://online.wsj.com/articles/
SB10001424052702303824204579421063632222426

Touchard, Laurent, "Niger: Les enjeux de la coopération sécuritaire avec la France," *Jeune Afrique*, March 3, 2014. As of November 12, 2014:
http://www.jeuneafrique.com/Article/ARTJAWEB20140303165915/

Transparency International, "Corruption by Country/Territory: Mali," undated (a); referenced July 14, 2014. As of November 12, 2014:
http://www.transparency.org/country#MLI

———, "Corruption Perceptions Index 2013," undated (b); referenced April 2014. As of November 17, 2014:
http://www.transparency.org/cpi2013/results

Traore, Seydou Moussa, Assa Gakou Doumbia, Vinima Traore, and Daniel Fassa Tolno, *4ème recensement général de la population et de l'habitat du Mali (RPGH-2009): Analyse des résultats définitifs*, Thème 2: *État et structure de la population*, République du Mali, Ministère de l'économie et des finances, Institut national de la statistique, Bureau central du recensement, December 2011. As of November 17, 2014:
http://www.instat.gov.ml/documentation/Rapport_Etat_Structure_VF.pdf

Trotha, Trutz von, and Georg Klute, "Von der Postkolonie zur Parastaatlichkeit: Das Beispiel Schwarzafrika," *Jahrbuch für internationale Sicherheitspolitik*, 2001. As of November 12, 2014:
http://www.bmlv.gv.at/wissen-forschung/publikationen/beitrag.php?id=611

Tuareg cultural association president, interview with Michael Shurkin, Bamako, October 8, 2013.

Tuareg leader and former high-level Malian government official, interview with Michael Shurkin, October 5, 2013.

Tuareg notable, phone interview with Michael Shurkin, October 4, 2013.

UNDP—*See* United Nations Development Programme.

United Nations Children's Fund, "Country Statistics," updated May 8, 2003. As of November 12, 2014:
http://www.unicef.org/statistics/index_countrystats.html

United Nations Development Programme, "In Paris, Niger Mobilizes $4.8 Billion for Development," November 16, 2012. As of November 12, 2014:
http://www.undp.org/content/undp/en/home/presscenter/articles/2012/11/16/a-paris-le-niger-mobilise-4-8-milliards-pour-le-d-veloppement/

———, *Sustaining Human Progress: Reducing Vulnerabilities and Building Resilience*, New York, July 2014. As of November 12, 2014:
http://hdr.undp.org/en/2014-report

United Nations Office on Drugs and Crime, *World Drug Report, 2013*, New York, May 2013. As of November 12, 2014:
http://www.unodc.org/wdr2013/

United Nations Security Council, *Report of the Assessment Mission on the Impact of the Libyan Crisis on the Sahel Region, 7 to 23 December 2011*, New York, S/2012/42, January 18, 2012. As of November 12, 2014:
http://www.un.org/Docs/journal/asp/ws.asp?m=S/2012/42

U.S. Department of State, "Chapter 2: Country Reports—Africa Overview," in *Country Reports on Terrorism 2013*, April 2014, pp. 11–228. As of November 12, 2014:
http://www.state.gov/j/ct/rls/crt/2013/224820.htm

Whitlock, Craig, "Drone Base in Niger Gives U.S. a Strategic Foothold in West Africa," *Washington Post*, March 21, 2013. As of November 12, 2014:
http://www.washingtonpost.com/world/national-security/drone-base-in-niger-gives-us-a-strategic-foothold-in-west-africa/2013/03/21/700ee8d0-9170-11e2-9c4d-798c073d7ec8_story.html

Wild, Rosa, "Security and Insecurity in Niger," *Think Africa Press*, November 11, 2011. As of November 12, 2014:
http://thinkafricapress.com/niger/security-insecurity-mercenaries

Wing, Susanna D., *Mali's Precarious Democracy and the Causes of Conflict*, Washington, D.C.: United States Institute of Peace, April 19, 2013. As of November 12, 2014:
http://www.usip.org/publications/mali-s-precarious-democracy-and-the-causes-of-conflict

Wing, Susanna D., and Bréhima Kassibo, "Mali: Incentives and Challenges for Decentralization," in James Tyler Dickovick and James S. Wunsch, eds., *Decentralization in Africa: The Paradox of State Strength*, Boulder, Colo.: Lynne Rienner Publishers, 2014.

World Bank, "Country Data Report for Mali, 1996–2012," c. 2013; referenced July 14, 2014.

Wulf, Eric, and Farley Mesko, *Guide to a Post-Conflict Mali*, Washington, D.C.: C4ADS, 2013.